# *The People of*
# PERTH AND KINROSS
## 1800 - 1850

### By
### David Dobson

CLEARFIELD

Copyright © 2021
by David Dobson
All Rights Reserved

Published for Clearfield Company by
Genealogical Publishing Company
Baltimore, Maryland
2021

ISBN 9780806359359

# INTRODUCTION

This book identifies people resident in the adjacent counties of Perthshire and Kinross-shire, as well people abroad who originated there, between 1800 and 1850. Perthshire is divided by a geological fault, known as the Highland Line, with Highland Perthshire to the northwest and Lowland Perthshire to the southeast, while Kinross-shire lies between Perthshire and the county of Fife. The two counties now form a unitary administrative unit, known as Perth and Kinross, centred on the city of Perth. The information found in the volume is derived from a wide range of archival sources such as court records, contemporary newspapers and journals, monumental inscriptions, and other documents. The entries connect emigrants, their destinations--especially in North America, the West Indies, and Australasia--with their kin who remained in Scotland.

The Statistical Report of Scotland, known as the O.S.A, is a collection of reports by nearly one thousand parish ministers in Scotland, compiled between 1791 and 1799 at the initiative of Sir John Sinclair. These reports cover a wide range of topics for each parish, including geography, education, history, agriculture, shipping, population, and religious denominations. The O.S.A. is a unique source of useful background for the family historian as it provides an insight into Scottish society at the end of the eighteenth century. Subsequent rapid changes in Scottish society brought about by the agricultural revolution and Industrial revolution, however, resulted in a call for the New Statistical Report being researched between 1832 and 1845. The agricultural revolution led to the formation of larger farms causing the surplus rural population to drift to the rapidly expanding factory towns. For example, in Perthshire the land-loom weavers who produced textiles in their home were replaced by textile mills, in towns like Stanley. The population of the city of Perth grew by 19,000 between 1755 and 1821, while that of Blairgowrie increased almost tenfold in the same period.

Both the O.S.A. and New Statistical Report were published, and copies may be found in most of the older libraries in Scotland; moreover, they are both available online on the website of the National Library of Scotland. This should enable researchers with roots in Perthshire and Kinross-shire to put their families—like the ones named in this book--into a historical context.

David Dobson

Dundee, Scotland, 2021

REFERENCES

AJ   Aberdeen Journal, series

AMC   Annals of Megantic County

ANY   St Andrew' Society of New York

AP   St Andrew's Society of Philadelphia

BA   Officers of the Bengal Army, 1758-1834

BM   Blackwood's Magazine, series

CCMC   Colonial Clergy of the Middle Colonies

CM   Caledonian Mercury, series

CGS   Campbells of Glengarry, Stormont and Harrington

DA   Dundee Advertiser, series

DCA   Dundee City Archives

DCB   Dictionary of Canadian Biography

DPCA   Dundee, Perth & Cupar Advertiser, series

DRTL   Daughters of the Republic of Texas Library

EA   Edinburgh Advertiser, series

EC   Edinburgh Courant, series

EEC   Edinburgh Evening Courant, series

F   Fasti Ecclesiae Scoticanae

FH   Fife Herald, series

FFP   Fife Free Press, series

FPF   Four Perthshire Families, Edinburgh, 1887

GC   Glasgow Courier, series

HBRS   Hudson Bay Record Society

IJ   Inverness Journal, series

Imm.NE   Immigrants, Salem, 1931

KCA   King's College, Aberdeen

LCL   Leith Commercial Lists, series

LER   Leith Episcopal Records

LGR   London Guildhall Records

MAGU   Matriculation Album, Glasgow University

MCA   Marischal College, Aberdeen

NARA   National Archives Records Administration

NCSA   North Carolina State Archives

NEHGS   New England Historic Genealogy Society

NLS   National Library of Scotland

NRS   National Records of Scotland

NSARM   Nova Scotia Archives & Records Management

PAC   Public Archives of Canada

PANB   Public Archives of New Brunswick

PKA   Perth and Kinross Archives

PL   Port of Leith

S   The Scotsman, series

SCA   South Carolina Archives

SG   Scottish Guardian, series

Sgen   Scottish Genealogist, series

SM   Scots Magazine, series

SRA   Strathclyde Regional Archives

TNA   The National Archives, London

TV   Tay Valley Family History Society

UNC   University of North Carolina

UPC   United Presbyterian Church

VaGaz   Virginia Gazette, series

XEBR   Extracts from Edinburgh Burgh Records

W   The Witness, series

ZA   Zealand Archives

River Tay and Kinnoull Hill

Scone Palace

Bridge over the North Inch at Perth

Dunblane Cathedral

Castle Menzies. View from South-East

# THE PEOPLE OF PERTH AND KINROSS, 1800-1850

ADAM, GEORGE, a blacksmith and locksmith in Perth in 1795. [NRS.GD1.427.16/6]

ADAM, HENRY, son of Andrew Adam a merchant in Errol, a prisoner in Perth Tolbooth, was accused of housebreaking and theft in 1820. [NRS.JC26.1820.10]

ADAMS, HENRY, born 1809 in Errol, a brickmaker and builder in Glasgow was accused of rape in 1850. [NRS.AD14.50.62]

ADAM, JOHN, son of John Adam at the Bridgend of Perth, was apprenticed to George Ralph and George Adam, blacksmiths and locksmiths in Perth in 1795 for five years. [NRS.GD1.427.16/6]

ADAMSON, Reverend JAMES, possibly from Monzie, was at the Cape of Good Hope, South Africa, in 1846. [NRS.S/H]

ADIE, WILLIAM, born 1829 in Milnathort, Kinross, was accused of robbery in Edinburgh in 1850. [NRS.AD14.50.5]

ALEXANDER, JAMES, born 1788, son of William Alexander in Ballairdrie, was accused of fire raising at the Lint Mill of Kirkton of Abernyte in 1801. [NRS.JC26.1801.48/5]

ALEXANDER, JOHN, of Netherton, a surgeon in Crieff, versus Reverend Samuel Cameron minister in Monzie, 1820. [NRS.CS228.A9.5]

ALEXANDER, WILLIAM, a merchant in Stanley, died 4 September 1865. [NRS.S/H.1882]

ALLAN, ELIZABETH, wife of David Halley a distiller in Crieff, versus John Mcintosh late gardener at Abercairney now in Foulis Wester, 1827. [NRS.CS97.H1.15]

ALLAN, HUGH, a vagrant and a thief in Perth Tolbooth, was banished from Scotland for 7 years, at Perth in 1793. [PKA.B59.26.11.2]

ALLAN, JOHN LEE, in Errol, father of Charles Edward Allan who died in Quebec on 4 July 1885. [DCA.3540]

ALLAN, SARAH, daughter of Alexander Allan in Abernethy, a victim of crime in 1823. [NRS.JC26.1823.198]

ALLAN, WILLIAM, born 1839, a stonecutter from Crieff, died at the home of his brother James Allan in Baxter, Gaspar County, Iowa, on 28 May 1879. [S.11207]

ALLAN WILLIAM, in South Street, Perth, a victim of embezzlement in 1849. [NRS.AD14.49.93]

ANDERSON, ALEXANDER, born 1772, a labourer from Fortingall, with his wife Isobel born 1776, son John born 1798, daughter Ann born 1800, daughter Christian born 1802, and daughter Isabel born 1804, emigrated aboard the Clarendon of Hull bound for Prince Edward Island in August 1808. [NSARM] [TNA.CO226.23]

ANDERSON, AMELIA, in Hawkhill, Kinross, the victim of arson in 1830. [NRS.AD14.30.356]

ANDERSON, CHARLES ENVERDALE, born 1838, sometime Provost of Coupar Angus, died in New York on 2 January 1902. [Coupar Angus gravestone]

ANDERSON, DAVID, agent in Coupar Angus for the Western Bank of Scotland, versus Major John Pennycook in 1835. [NRS.CS271.64157]

ANDERSON, DUNCAN, in Killin, a letter re his brother Ronald Anderson, who had died in Jamaica, 1806. [NRS.GD112.11.7.9.20]

ANDERSON, DUNCAN, with two children, from Comrie, emigrated via Greenock aboard the Curlew bound for Quebec on 21 July 1818. [TNA.CO384/3.123-127]

ANDERSON, GEORGE, a feuar and wright in Stanley, died in October 1832, father of Thomas Anderson an insurance clerk in New Orleans. [NRS.S/H]

ANDERSON, GEORGE, a turner in Perth, died 27 March 1859, father of James Anderson in Portland, Maine. [NRS.S/H.1888]

ANDERSON, JAMES, an Excise officer in Doune, having seized a cartload of illicit whisky was assaulted in 1803. [NRS.JC26.1803.6]

ANDERSON, JAMES, of the Commercial Bank in Blairgowrie, versus James Morrison in 1837, [NRS.CS271.59145]; also, versus John Gilbert, in 1839 [NRS.CS271.36004]; a banker in Blairgowrie, a trustee in 1842. [NRS.CS96.4395]

ANDERSON, JOHN, born 1781, son of John Anderson, a farmer in Easter Buchanty, and his wife Ann Moir, [1750-1801], died in Honduras in March 1813. [Monzie gravestone]

ANDERSON, JOHN, with his wife Isabella and six children, from Kenmore, emigrated via Greenock aboard the Sophia of Ayr bound for Quebec on 26 July 1818. [TNA.CO384/3.133-134]

ANDERSON, Dr JOHN, son of John Anderson the Collector of Excise in Perth, died at Oak Ridges, Richmond Hill, Toronto, Canada, on 19 November 1843. [EEC.20987]

ANDERSON, PETER, with his wife Christine and six children, from Kenmore, emigrated via Greenock aboard the Sophia of Ayr bound for Quebec on 26 July 1818. [TNA.CO384/3.133-134]

ANDERSON, LESLIE, a weaver in Easter Greenside, imprisoned in Perth Tolbooth, a petition, 1810. [PKA.B59.39.2.83]

ANDERSON, WALTER, from Dunkeld, father of a daughter born in Pittsburgh, Pennsylvania, on 16 September 1868. [S.7860]

ANDERSON, WILLIAM, born 1783, from Aberdalgie emigrated via Stornaway on the Prince of Wales to the Hudson Bay Company settlement on the Red River in 1811. [PAC.M155.145]

ANDERSON, WILLIAM, Depute Manager of the Oriental Bank in Calcutta, India, in 1849. [NRS.S.C. Perth.49/91]

ANDERSON, WILLIAM, a minister in Auchterarder, died 8 May 1855. [NRS.S/H.1856]

ANNAND, ALEXANDER, at Mudhall Stables, Bendochy, a victim of theft in 1832. [NRS.AD14.32.28]

ANNAN, ROBERT, surgeon in Kinross, versus James Skelton of Orwall, 1823. [NRS.CS228.A9.21]

ARCHER, WILLIAM, born 1778 in Perthshire, died in Savanna, Georgia, on 18 October 1805. [Savanna Death Register]

AULD, ROBERT THOMAS, minister at Moneydie, a letter, 1849. [NRS.GD155.1128]

AYSON, WILLIAM J., in Blairgowrie, a sequestration petition, 1846. [NRS.CS279.130]

AYTON, ROGER JAMES, son of Captain Ayton in Glendevon, to obtain a commission in the army in 1842. [NRS.GD1.678.38]

BAILLIE, WALTER, foreman at Argaith, Errol, was accused of theft in 1831. [NRS.AD14.31.55]

BAIN, JAMES, born 1802 in Madderty, son of Peter Bain an articifier, educated at Glasgow University, emigrated to Canada in 1854, a minister in Ontario from 1854 to 1874, died in Markham, Ontario, on 9 December 1885. [F.7.625] NRS.AD14.33.12]

BAIN, MARGARET, wife of Alexander McIntyre a labourer at Battlefield, Redgorton, accused of housebreaking and theft in 1822. [NRS.AD14.22.121]

BAIN, PETER, born 1801, a butcher in Dunblane, was accused of sheep stealing in 1833. [NRS.AD14]

BAIRD, JANET, in Tarbolton, Canada, in 1846. [NRS.S.C.Perth.46.511]

BAIRD, JOHN, a mason in Errol, accounts with the heritors of Longforgan, 1825-1826. [NRS.GD508.6.14]

BAKER, JAMES, a merchant in Philadelphia, Pennsylvania, in 1822. [NRS.S.C.Perth.17.77]

BALFOUR, JAMES, a drover from Callander, accused of theft, 1819. [NRS.AD14.19.39]

BALFOUR, JOHN, a slater in Doune, Kilmadock, accused of hamesucken, assault, and theft in 1818. [NRS.AD14.18.88]

BALLANTYNE, ISABELLA, died on 17 January 1861 in North America. [Perth, Greyfriars, gravestone]

BALLANTYNE, JAMES, in Dunblane, was accused of discharging a firearm and theft in 1824. [NRS.AD14.24.364]

BALLANTYNE, JAMES, in Perth, 1829, heir to his brother Robert Ballantine, a merchant in Albany, New York. [NRS.S/H]

BALLINGALL, JAMES, a cabinetmaker in Perth, uncle of James Ballingall in San Francisco, California. [NRS.S/H.1854]

BALLINGALL, JEAN, daughter of David Ballingall in Burnside of Wester Dron, versus James Greenhill, son of Peter Greenhill of Cordon of Strathearn, process of declarator of marriage, 1812. [NRS.CC8.6.1480]

BANCANKEL, JAMES, from Perthshire, emigrated via Liverpool to North America in June 1833. [SG.2.152]

BANNERMAN, ALEXANDER, son of Henry Bannerman in Perth, was apprenticed to Robert Peddie a writer there, in 1813. [PKA.B59.29.94]

BANNERMAN, ROBERT ALEXANDER, of Abernyte, papers, 1820-1825. [PKA.B59.38.5.67]

BARCLAY, HUGH, Sheriff Substitute of Perthshire, a victim of assault in 1831. [NRS.AD14.31.47]

BARCLAY, JOHN, in Tulloch, Perth, a victim of embezzlement in 1849. [NRS.AD14.49.93]

BARCLAY, ROBERT, master of the Margaret of Perth, from Dundee with passengers bound for Jamaica in 1815. [DPCA]

BARGLASS, WILLIAM, a servant in Clathiemore, a murderer, was sentenced to transportation on 27 September 1800. [PKA.B59.26.11.2]

BARLAND, JOHN, tacksman of Stormontfield, died 7 December 1827, father of Thomas Barland settled in Wisconsin before 1862. [NRS.S/H.1862]

BARNET, DAVID, a labourer in Auchterarder, residing in Newton of Pitcairn, Dunning, was accused of operating an illicit still at Baulk of Struie, and assaulting Dugald Cameron an Excise officer in 1818. [NRS.JC26.1819.145.60]]

BARNET, JAMES, a quarrier in Mylnefield, Longforgan, a rioter in 1831. [NRS.AD14.31.378]

BARR, FIDELE, in Milnathort, a victim of theft and fraud in 1846. [NRS.JC26.1847.637]

BARRY, CHARLES HENDERSON, in Jefferson, New York, by 1845. [NRS.Perth.SC]

BARRIE, JAMES, born 1785 in Moneydie, died in Savanna, Georgia, on 10 October 1817. [Savanna gravestone]

BARTY, THOMAS, a writer in Dunblane, accounts, 1831-1840. [NRS.GD24.1.730]

BATTISON, PETER, in Tulloch, Balquhidder, 1812. [NRS.CS233.SEQNS.BI.39]

BAXTER, JOHN, born 1788, died 26 December 1853, husband of Susan Roberts, born 1784, died 21 May 1858, parents of John Baxter farmer at Blackhill. [Meigle gravestone]

BAXTER, JOHN, at Mudhall Stables, Bendochy, a victim of theft in 1832. [NRS.AD14.32.28]

BAXTER, THOMAS, and his wife Janet Wilson, parents of George Baxter, born 1854, died 1885 in Silvertown, New South Wales, in 1885. [Newburgh gravestone]

BAYNE, JAMES, a farmer in Buttergask, was granted lands in Blackford in 1814. [NRS.GD24.1.93.1]

BAYNE, JANET, daughter of James Bayne, [1822-1898], and his wife Ann McKenzie, [died 1909], wife of William Kirton, died in Calgary, Alberta, on 8 April 1901. [Dunblane gravestone]

BEATH, GEORGE, a mason in Kinnesswood, was murdered on 28 July 1802. [NRS.JC26.1803.14]

BEATON, DONALD, in Vaughan, York, Canada, in 1860. [NRS.S.C.Perth.61.101]

BEATSON, GEORGE, born 1849, son of John Beatson a miller in Abernethy, died in Trenton, New Jersey, on 4 August 1873. [S.9385]

BELL, JAMES, a cattle drover in Coupar Angus, accused of theft in 1802, transported for seven years. [NRS.AD14.12.40; JC11.40]

BELL, JESSIE, probably from Bridge of Earn, settled in Quebec by 1832. [NRS.GD1.1045.3]

BELL, WILLIAM, born 1789, a labourer from Methven, emigrated via Greenock on the William of New York bound for New York on 4 September 1817, arrived there on 17 October 1817. [NY Municipal Archives] [NY Commercial Advertiser, 18.10.1817]

BENNETT, JOHN, in Kepp, Dunblane, was accused of hamesucken in 1825. [NRS.AD14.25.248]

BENNETT, PETER, from Gairney Bridge, Kinross, died on Leyden Estate, St James, Jamaica, on 14 July 1823. [S.395.679]

BETT, JOHN, born 1825 in Coupar Angus, son of William Bett, settled on Staten Island, New York, in 1864, died in St Andrews, Fife, on 14 March 1910. [ANY.2.273]

BETT, WILLIAM, agent in Coupar Angus of the Perth Banking Company, and trustee of Alexander Batley deceased, in 1815. [NRS.CS36.13.24]

BIRRELL, JAMES, in Emerald Hill, Melbourne, Australia, 1865. [NRS.S.C.Perth.66.14]

BISSET, ANN, born 1803, daughter of John Bisset a mason and vintner in Bankhead, Blairgowrie, accused of theft in 1841. [NRS.AD14.41.210]

BISSET, THOMAS, in Guiana, 1815. [NRS.S.C.Perth.10.177]

BLACK, ALEXANDER, born 1814, from Perth, died in Montreal on 15 February 1869. [S.7987]

BLACK, GEORGE, in Melbourne, Victoria, Australia, 1858. [NRS.S.C.Perth.59.158]

BLACK, PETER, a mason in Crieff, died May 1849. [NRS.S/H]

BLACK, THOMAS, in Forenaught, Fowlis Wester, accused of fraud, outlawed on 6 May 1806. [NRS.JC11.48]

BLACKWOOD, or BLACKET, JAMES, son of John Blackwood a labourer in Crook of Devon, accused of assault in 1824. [NRS.AC14.24.68]

BLACKWOOD, ROBERT, from Kinross, a theological student in 1811, emigrated to America in 1816, a minister in Nova Scotia, died 12 December 1857. [UPC]

BLAIKIE, PETER, son of David Blaikie a farmer in Little Dunkeld, was apprenticed to John Blaikie his brother, a plumber in Aberdeen, from 1785 to 1792. [ACA]

BLAIR, ADAM JOHNSTON FERGUSON, from Balthayock, Perthshire, President of Privy Council of Canada, died in Ottawa on 29 December 1867. [S.7632]

BLAIR, or GLASS, ANN, in Bonhard, Scone, was accused of theft in 1832. [NRS.AD14.32.96]

BLAIR, CHARLES, and John Blair merchants in Dunkeld, sons of the deceased Charles Blair a merchant in Dunkeld, and William Blair a manufacturer in Perth, son of the deceased John Blair a merchant in Perth, versus James Charles Blair in Perth, 1834. [NRS.CS228.B17.105]

BLAIR, CHRISTINE ROBERTSON, wife of Laurence Oliphant of Gask, a tack of Woodside of Ardblair, Kinloch, to John Bell for fifteen years in 1815. [PKA.B59.38.6.264]

BLAIR, GEORGE, born 1818 in Perth, was educated at the University of St Andrews in 1835, a school superintendent in Canada, a missionary in the Alleghany Mountains of USA, died in February 1897. [F.7.627]

BLAIR, THOMAS, a merchant in Alyth, died 3 January 1810. [NRS.S/H.1855]

BOAG, MARGARET, sister of William Boag a weaver in Dunning, and daughter of John Boag a labourer in Dunning, accused of murder, theft and reset in 1823. [NRS.AD14.2311; 2450]

BOLT, LAWRENCE, a sergeant of the North Lowland Fencible Regiment in Perth, accused of murder but not proven in 1802. [NRS.JC11.40]

BONAR, ANDREW A., minister of the Free Church in Collace, a petition, 1845. [NRS.GD112.51.186]

BOOSIE, ANDREW, chairman of the Milnathort Free Church, a petition, 1845. [NRS.GD112.51.189]

BOYD, BARBARA, born 1802, daughter of Thomas Boyd, farmer at the Mains of Megginch, Errol, and his wife Barbara Drummond, was accused of theft in 1832. [NRS.AD14.32.121]

BOYD, or ANDERSON, ELIZABETH, a widow in Newburgh, daughter of Thomas Boyd, farmer at the Mains of Megginch, Errol, and his wife Barbara Drummond, was accused of theft in 1832. [NRS.AD14.32.121]

BRADDOCK, EDWARD, born 1695 in Perthshire, an army officer, to America in 1755. [WA]

BRAE, MARGARET, daughter of Patrick Brae vintner at the Bridgend of Tay, widow of George Thomson a Customs House clerk in Perth, 20 May 1818. [NRS.GD1.406.25]

BRAKENRIDGE, DAVID, a surgeon in the Service of the Honourable East India Company, later in Perth by 1869. [NRS.S.C.Perth.69.100]

BRYDIE, JAMES, farmer in Gatherleys, versus William Morrison farmer in Rossie, Andrew McIntyre sheriff officer in Dunning, and Thomas Wright a messenger at arms in Dunning, in 1827. [NRS.CS228.B1724]

BRIDIE, ROBERT, born 1784, a cooper from Perth, was naturalised in South Carolina on 13 September 1807. [NARA.M1183.1]

BRIGGS, AGNES, wife of Alexander Smith in Perth, dead by 1855, mother of Agnes Smith or De Blaquire, and Andrew Smith in Canada. [NRS.S/H]

BRODIE, ALICE LINDSAY, daughter of James Brodie in Perth, and wife of David Prophet a solicitor, died in St Kilda, Melbourne, Australia, on 18 September 1875. [AJ.6674]

BRODIE, AMELIA MARIA, daughter of James Brodie the city chamberlain of Perth, married John Cheetham of the Bank of Victoria, in St Kilda, Melbourne, Australia, on 10 April 1862. [AJ.5971]

BRODIE, JAMES, a merchant in Perth, business correspondence, 1812. [PKA.B59.37.3.2]

BRODIE, JAMES, in Perth, father of Alice Lindsay Brodie, wife of David Prophet a solicitor, died in St Kilda, Melbourne, Australia, on 18 September 1875. [AJ.6674]

BRODIE, JOHN, of Blackhill, papers, 1807-1815. [PKA.B59.38.6.245]

BRODIE, JOHN, born 1767 in Perthshire, a slater, with his wife Elizabeth Archibald, daughter Lindsay born 1798, and sons John born 1800, and James born 1802, emigrated via Liverpool to New York, was naturalised there on 15 November 1819. [NARA]

BROUGH, JAMES, in South Clutha, Otago, New Zealand, 1856. [NRS.S.C.Perth.56.260]

BROWN, CHARLES, a founder in Perth prison accused of theft, was sentenced to transportation for ten years on 10 September 1799. [NRS.JC11.44]

BROWN, DAVID, born 1801, son of Gilbert Brown and his wife Ann Williamson, died in Tasmania on 28 February 1889. [Abernethy gravestone]

BROWN, EDWARD, a merchant, 22 Gore Street, Melbourne, in 1875. [NRS.S.C.Perth.74.162]

BROWN, GEORGE, a carter in Blairdrummond, accused of hamesucken, assault, and theft in 1818. [NRS.AD14.18.88]

BROWN, GEORGE, in Oararm, Otago, New Zealand, 1875. [NRS.S.C.Perth.90.87]

BROWN, GEORGE, possibly from Perth, a surveyor at 157 Broadway Street, New York, in 1852, formerly in Quebec, Montreal, Connecticut, and Long Island, a letter. [PKA.ms85, bundle 85]

BROWN, GILBERT, born 1807, son of Gilbert Brown and his wife Ann Williamson, died in Tarraville, Gippsland, Victoria, on 25 December 1878. [Abernethy gravestone]

BROWN, JOHN, from Milnathort, a theological student in 1790, a missionary in America in 1795, later a minister in Londonderry, Nova Scotia. [UPC]

BROWN, JOHN, in Dunning, was accused of operating an illicit still at Baulk of Struie, and assaulting Dugald Cameron an Excise officer in 1818. [NRS.JC26.1819.18]

BROWN, JOHN, born 1807, son of Reverend William Brown, [1774-1829], and his wife Christine Whyte, [1775-1862], died at Montego Bay, Jamaica, on 24 January 1845. [Greyfriars gravestone, Perth]

BROWN, LAURENCE B., born 1836, died in Mexico on 21 September 1904.

BROWN, MALCOLM, born in Kinross, a shoemaker, accused of housebreaking and theft in 1832. [NRS.AD14.32.30]

BROWN, MARGARET, alias Elizabeth Robertson, alias Mar.garet McVey or McPhail, a vagrant and fortune teller, was banished in Perth on 24 September 1793. [PKA.B59.26.11.2]

BROWN, ROBERT, born 1767, formerly of Perth Nurseries, died in Philadelphia on 20 September 1845. [EEC.21257][W.616]

BROWN, WILLIAM, born 25 March 1781 in Alyth, son of John Brown and his wife Margaret Haldane, emigrated to Iowa in 1820, married Margaret Main, died in Keokuk, Iowa, on 22 September 1821. [FPF]

BROWN, WILLIAM, a labourer in Gilmerton, accused of theft in 1827. [NRS.JC26.1827.392]

BRUCE, or HAZELS, ALEXANDER, born 1817, a labourer in Blairgowrie, was accused of theft in 1832. [NRS.AD14.32.130]

BRUCE, ALEXANDER, a mason in Burrelton, died 11 February 1847, father of Lawrence Bruce in St Louis. [NRS.S/H.1866]

BRUCE, or HAZELS, HENRY, born 1813, a labourer in Blairgowrie, was accused of theft in 1832. [NRS.AD14.32.130]

BRUCE, LAURENCE B., born 1836, died in Mexico on 21 September 1904. [Cargill gravestone]

BRUCE, MARGARET, born 1800, daughter of Charles Bruce in the Mains of Kilgraston, married Patrick Thomson a merchant, died in New York on 11 July 1822. [DPCA]

BRUCE, ROBERT, from Balbeggie, a theological student in 1802, graduated as a Doctor of Divinity, emigrated to America as a minister, later was President of Pittsburgh University in Pennsylvania. [UPC]

BRUCE, ROBERT, son of George Bruce a butcher in Errol, a prisoner in Perth Tolbooth, was accused of housebreaking and theft in 1820. [NRS.JC26.1820.10]

BRUCE, WILLIAM, a victual dealer in Dunning, accused of forgery in 1834. [NRS.AD14.34.311]

BRUCE, WILLIAM M., born 1844, died in Warrenburg, USA, on 17 March 1892. [Cargill gravestone]

BRYCE, ARCHIBALD, in Doune, Kilmadock, with a cartload of illicit whisky, assaulted Excisemen attempting to arrest him in 1803. [NRS.JC26.1803.6]

BRYCE, GRIZEL, in Blackford, was accused of concealing a pregnancy, was sentence to nine months imprisonment in Perth Tolbooth, 1820. [NRS.JC26.1820.112]; widow of William Headrick a publican in Blackford, accused of robbery in 1820. [NRS.AD14.20.196]

BRYDIE, JEAN, from Perth, settled in Charleston, South Carolina, before 1798. [NRS.CS17.1.17/33]

BRYDIE, ROBERT, a merchant from Perth, settled in Charleston, South Carolina, before 1798. [NRS.CS17.1.17/33]

BRYSON, CHRISTIAN, born 1793 in Chapelhill, Moneydie, emigrated via Greenock on 4 September 1817 on the William of New York bound for New York, landed there on 17 October 1817. [NY Municipal Archives] [NY Commercial Advertiser, 18.10.1817].

BRYSON, JAMES, born 1794 in Chapelhill, Moneydie, a labourer, emigrated via Greenock on 4 September 1817 on the William of New York bound for New York, landed there on 17 October 1817. [NY Municipal Archives][NY Commercial Advertiser, 18.10.1817].

BRYSON, ROBERT, born 1787 in Chapelhill, Moneydie, a labourer, emigrated via Greenock on 4 September 1817 on the William of New York bound for New York, landed there on 17 October 1817. [NY Municipal Archives][NY Commercial Advertiser, 18.10.1817].

BRYSON, ROBERT, born 1787, a labourer, with his wife Elizabeth, born 1795, and daughter Jean born 1815, from House of Burn, Monyvaird, emigrated via Greenock on 4 September 1817 on the William of New York bound for New York, landed there on 17 October 1817. [NY Municipal Archives] [NY Commercial Advertiser, 18.10.1817].

BUCHAN, ALEXANDER, in Perth Tolbooth, was accused of housebreaking and theft, was sentenced to transportation beyond the seas for seven years in 1819. [NRS.JC26.1819.85]

BUCHAN, DUNCAN, a miller at Kilmahog, Callendar, was found guilty of assault and sentenced to six months imprisonment in 1819. [NRS.JC11.60]

BUCHAN, ISAAC, a mason in Doune, Kilmadock, was assaulted by spirit smugglers in 1808. [NRS.JC26.1808.7]

BUCHAN, JAMES, in Perth Tolbooth accused of theft in 1827. [NRS.JC26.1827.392]

BUCHANAN, DONALD, born 1794, a labourer from Kenmore, emigrated via Port Glasgow aboard the Favourite of St John bound for St John, New Brunswick, on 22 October 1815. [PANB.ms23E.9798]

BUCHANAN, FRANCIS, a shoemaker in Doune, Kilmadock, was accused of hamesucken, assault, and theft in 1818. [NRS.AD14.18.88]

BUCHANAN, GEORGE, born in Perthshire, emigrated to Canada, minister in Beckwith, Ontario, from 1822 until his death in 1835. [F.VII.628]

BUCHANAN, JAMES, born 1791, a labourer from Kenmore, emigrated via Port Glasgow aboard the Favourite of St John bound for St John, New Brunswick, on 22 October 1815. [PANB.ms23E.9798]

BUCHANAN, PETER, born in Perthshire, was naturalised in South Carolina on 10 February 1818. [S.C. State Records.04.278]

BUCHANAN, ROBERT, born 1794, a labourer from Balquhidder, emigrated via Port Glasgow aboard the Favourite of St John bound for St John, New Brunswick, on 22 October 1815. [PANB.ms23E.9798]

BUCHANAN, THOMAS, a hostler in Deanston, Kilmadock, was accused of theft in 1839. [NRS.AD14.39.76]

BUIST, GEORGE, a saddle and harness maker in Perth, 1805. [NRS.GD1.427.16/8]

BULLIONS, ALEXANDER, from Logiealmond, a theological student in 1802, graduated DD, a missionary in America, a minister in Cambridge, New York, later a Professor of Theology. [UPC]

BULLIONS, JAMES, born 1779, from Perthshire, emigrated via Port Glasgow aboard the Commerce bound for Pictou, Nova Scotia, on 10 August 1803. [NLS.ms1053.104-109]

BULLIONS, PETER, born 1790 in Logiealmond, a theological student in 1813, a minister in Argyle, Washington County, and later in Troy, New York, died 14 February 1863. [UPC]

BURDEN, HENRY, born 22 April 1791 in Dunblane, son of Peter Burden and his wife Elizabeth Abercrombie, settled in Troy, New York, in 1819, died in 1871. [BLG.2591]

BURGOYNE, CHARLES, born 1828, an iron wire worker in Coupar Angus, was accused of assaulting an officer of the law in 1849. [NRS.AD14.49.299]

BURNS, DAVID, and John Burns manufacturers in Perth, also David Burns a farmer in Kinclaven, versus John Syme, cashier of the Union Bank of Perth in 1814. [NRS.CS40.17.19]

BURNS, JOHN, with his wife and two children, from Rattray, emigrated via Greenock aboard the Portaferry bound for Quebec in May 1832. [Quebec Mercury, 13.6.1832]

BURNTFIELD, DAVID, born 1808, son of George Burntfield and his wife Lillie Stewart, died in Dominica, British West Indies, on 4 June 1838. [Greyfriars gravestone, Perth]

BUTTER, ELIZABETH, daughter of James Butter from Perth, married Captain John Macintosh, in Toronto on 10 March 1834. [DPCA.1659]

CAIRNS, JAMES MILN, born 1806 in Longforgan, son of Reverend Adam Cairns and his wife ....Miln, graduated from Glasgow University, a schoolmaster in New York, died 24 July 1832 in Peebles. [ANY]

CAIRNS, JAMES, a weaver in Auchterarder, dead by 1836, father of John Cairns in Sabinhill, New York. [NRS.S/H]

CAIRNS, JOHN, in Kippendavie, Dunblane, a sequestration petition, 1844. [NRS.CS279.367]

CAMERON, ALEXANDER, born 1796 in Perthshire, emigrated via Greenock on the Recovery bound for New York on 4 August 1803. [NLS.ms1053]

CAMERON, ALLAN, in Doune, was accused of assault in 1809. [NRS.JC26.1809.17]

CAMERON, or MENZIES, AMELIA, and her son James Menzies, merchants in Weem, sederunt book, 1798-1800. [NRS.CS96.3467]

CAMERON, ARCHIBALD COWIE, son of John Cameron the schoolmaster in Glen Lyon, Fortingall, graduated MA from Marischal College, Aberdeen, in 1845, later a schoolteacher in Fettercairn. [MCA]

CAMERON, DONALD, a schoolmaster in Aberfeldy in 1801, [NRS.GD112.11.7.4.18]; in Aberfeldy, a teacher who petitioned for a schoolroom there in 1822. [NRS.GD112.11.8.15.1]

CAMERON, DUNCAN, with his wife Mary and two children, from Dull, emigrated via Greenock aboard the Curlew bound for Quebec on 21 July 1818. [TNA.CO384/3.123-127]

CAMERON, FINDLAY, with his wife Janet, from Dull, emigrated via Greenock aboard the Curlew bound for Quebec on 21 July 1818. [TNA.CO384/3.123-127]

CAMERON, GEORGE S., born 1815 in Perthshire, a merchant in Charleston, South Carolina, was naturalised on 23 December 1838. [NARA.M1183.1]

CAMERON, HENRY, the stamp-master in Errol in 1801, [NRS.GD508.9.34/15]; stamp-master in Errol and Inchture a letter 1801, [NRS.GD508.9.34]; a manufacturer in Errol, a bond of caution for Thomas Scott a farmer and innkeeper at Errol Milne, 1803. [NRS.CS271.542]

CAMERON, HUGH PERCY, born 1817, son of Alexander Cameron, [1776-1831], and his wife Mary Davidson, [1779-1858], died in Charleston, South Carolina, on 18 September 1854. [Little Dunkeld gravestone]

CAMERON, JAMES, born 1774 in Perthshire, a grocer in New York, died on 22 January 1851. [ANY]

CAMERON, Dr JAMES, born 1785 in Kinross, son of James Cameron, [1752-1832], and his wife Magdalene Gordon, [1757-1830], settled in New York, died at 18 North Moore Street, N.Y., on 12 December 1851. [Milnathort gravestone, Kinross] [W.XIII.1291] [ANY]

CAMERON, JAMES, a merchant in Dunkeld, and agent for the Perth Union Bank, was accused of forgery in 1824. [NRS.AD14.24.104]

CAMERON, JAMES, born 1808, son of Alexander Cameron and his wife Mary Davidson, died in Demerara on 10 June 1840. [Little Dunkeld gravestone]

CAMERON, JOHN, son of John Cameron in Lag of Grantully, was apprenticed to James Young a clock and watchmaker in Perth for four years, in 1795. [NRS.GD1.427.16/5]

CAMERON, JOHN, in Foveran, a decreet, 1800. [NRS.CS271.41133]

CAMERON, JOHN, from Kenmore, with his wife, sons John, Donald, and Ewen, emigrated via Fort William bound for Quebec in June 1802. [PAC.mg24.1183]

CAMERON, JOHN, from Glen Turret, emigrated via Fort William bound for Quebec in June 1802. [PAC.mg24.1183]

CAMERON, JOHN, in Aberfeldy, son of Donald Cameron the schoolmaster, a letter, 1803. [NRS.GD112.11.7.6.1]

CAMERON, JOHN, born 1782, a labourer from Kenmore, with his wife Margaret born 1788, and children Robert born 1805, Mary born 1807, Jean born 1809, and Peter born 1811, emigrated via Port Glasgow aboard the Favourite of St John bound for St John, New Brunswick, on 22 October 1815. [PANB.ms23E.9798]

CAMERON, JOHN, a labourer in Caullyfountain, Forteviot, was accused of bigamy in 1823. [NRS.AD14.23.218]

CAMERON, JOHN, MD, born in Kinross, died in North Moore Street, New York, in 1851. [S.17.1852]

CAMERON, MARY, servant to Duncan McFarlane, a tenant in Boreland of Ruskie, was accused of concealment of pregnancy in 1816. [NRS.JC26.1816.139]

CAMERON, THOMAS, in Wester Struan, Glen Quaich, with a licence to deal in whisky, in 1822. [NRS.GD112.11.8.14.23]

CAMPBELL, Major General ALEXANDER, a charter, 1816. [NRS.GD43.33.18]

CAMPBELL, ALEXANDER, born 1794, a labourer from Kincairn, emigrated via Port Glasgow aboard the Favourite of St John bound for St John, New Brunswick, on 22 October 1815. [PANB.ms23E.9798]; landed there in November 1815. [PANB.msRS555.C4]

CAMPBELL, ALEXANDER, from Killin, emigrated on the Harmony bound for Canada in 1817, settled in Mariposa, Ontario. [CGS.274]

CAMPBELL, ALEXANDER A., born 16 February 1823 in Auchterarder, a carpenter and builder, emigrated to Philadelphia, Pennsylvania, in May 1861, died there on 26 August 1903. [AP]

CAMPBELL, ARCHIBALD, Captain on half pay of the 56$^{th}$ Regiment, died in Perth on 5 May 1820. [SM.86.95]

CAMPBELL, ARCHIBALD, born 16 November 1779 in Glen Lyon, son of Donald Campbell and his wife Mary Campbell, settled in Albany, New York, died there on 14 July 1865. [CCS/USA]

CAMPBELL, ARCHIBALD, born 1813, son of Archibald Campbell, [1781-1843], a sawyer in Perth, and his wife Margaret Watt, [1791-1854], died in New Orleans, Louisiana, on 5 October 1839. [Perth, Greyfriars gravestone]

CAMPBELL, CATHERINE, wife of John Campbell a quarrier at Kendrum of Logie Almond, Monzie, a victim of housebreaking and theft in 1835. [NRS.AD14.35.108]

CAMPBELL, Captain CHARLES WILLIAM, of Boreland, Killin, was accused of culpable homicide in 1831. [NRS.AD14.31.70]

CAMPBELL, Colonel COLIN, Staff Officer of Pensioners in Perth, father of Amelia Ann Campbell who died in Clive Grange, Napier, New Zealand, wife of Hugh Handyside. [S.13001]

CAMPBELL, DAVID, son of Alexander and Janet Campbell, settled in Canada by 1869. [Killichonan gravestone, Fortingall]

CAMPBELL, DONALD, a house servant in Taymouth, a petition, 1815. [NRS.GD112.11.8.10.8]

CAMPBELL, DOUGAL, keeper of Dunblane Tolbooth 1807-1808. [PKA.B59.24.11.190]

CAMPBELL, DUNCAN, from Moerlanich, Breadalbane, emigrated to America in 1807. [NRS.GD119.11.8.2.17-18]

CAMPBELL, DUNCAN, from Comrie, a theological student in 1811, emigrated to America as a surgeon. [UPC]

CAMPBELL, DUNCAN, born 1771 near Loch Tay, husband of Catherine McIntyre, [1779-1873], emigrated to Canada in 1816, settled in Glengarry County, Ontario, died 1844. [CGS.204]

CAMPBELL, DUNCAN, born 1821, son of Archibald Campbell and his wife Christian Gow, settled in Fealar, New Zealand, died in Perth on 6 February 1900. [Fortingall Dunalister gravestone]

CAMPBELL, DUNCAN, a tenant in Croftnallin, Fearnan, a letter, 1828. [NRS.GD112.74.693.9/21]

CAMPBELL, DUNCAN, with his wife Catherine and three children, from Killin, emigrated via Greenock aboard the Curlew bound for Quebec on 21 July 1818. [TNA.CO384/3.123-127]

CAMPBELL, FINLAY, in Ballechroisk, Killin, bound for America in 1802. [NRS.GD112.11.7.5.15]

CAMPBELL, GEORGE, a weaver in Dunkeld, was accused of assault in 1822. [NRS.AD14.22.10]

CAMPBELL, HUGH PERCY, born 1817, son of Alexander Campbell, [1776-1831], and his wife Mary Davidson, [1779-1858], died in Charleston, South Carolina, on 18 September 1854. [Little Dunkeld gravestone]

CAMPBELL, IAN, born 1789, a thief who was sentenced to transportation to the colonies, at Perth on 5 October 1832. [PKA.B59.26.11]

CAMPBELL, JAMES, born 1791, a labourer from Killin, with his wife Mary born 1787, and children James born 1809, Alexander born 1811, and James born 1813, emigrated via Port Glasgow aboard the Favourite of St John bound for St John, New Brunswick, on 22 October 1815. [PANB.ms23E.9798]

CAMPBELL, JAMES, in Dunning, was accused of stealing sheep in 1827. [NRS.JC26.1827.392]

CAMPBELL, or MCLELLAN, JANET, in Dunning, was accused of murdering James McLellan, spouse of Janet Campbell, in 1846. [NRS.AD14.46.338]

CAMPBELL, JOHN, born 1758, a labourer from Rannoch, with his wife Catherine born 1763, daughter Catherine born 1788, daughter Margaret born 1790, daughter Isobel born 1792, daughter Mary born 1794, daughter Janet born 1797, daughter Elizabeth born 1799, son

Archibald born 1804, and daughter Christian born 1807, emigrated aboard the Clarendon of Hull bound for Prince Edward Island in August 1808. [NSARM] [TNA.CO226.23]

CAMPBELL, JOHN, born 1799, son of Donald Campbell and his wife Jessie Reid, died in Australia in 1853. [Fortingall Killochoman gravestone]

CAMPBELL, JOHN, from Killin, emigrated on the Harmony bound for Canada in 1817, settled in Galt, Ontario. [CGS.274]

CAMPBELL, JOHN, of Dubheads, Madderty, 1802. [NRS.GD112.39.387.10]

CAMPBELL, JOHN, with his wife Mary and six children, from Killin, emigrated via Greenock aboard the Sophia of Ayr bound for Quebec on 26 July 1818. [TNA.CO384/3.133-134]

CAMPBELL, JOHN, Excise officer in Killin, applied for a house there formerly occupied by Dr Campbell, in 1804. [NRS.GD112.11.7.7.25]

CAMPBELL, JOHN, son of John Campbell, a merchant in Perth, a planter in Grenada, testament, 1808, Comm. Edinburgh. [NRS]

CAMPBELL, MALCOLM, born 1772 in Killin, a stone-mason, husband of Ann Anderson, [1774-1856], emigrated on the Harmony bound for Canada in 1817, settled in Dominionville, Ontario, died 1864. [CGS.274]

CAMPBELL, MARK, from Dunkeld, died in Grenada on 2 December 1791. [EEC.24.3.1792]

CAMPBELL, MARY, born 1753 in Glen Lyon, daughter of Peter Campbell and his wife Margaret Stewart, married Donald Campbell, [1750-1782], emigrated to New York in 1798, died in York, Genessee County, N.Y., in 1823. [CCS]

CAMPBELL, PATRICK, of Achalader, Ballied, Blairgowrie, a letter, 1810. [NRS.GD51.341]

CAMPBELL, PETER, born in Killin, a vintner in Crieff, applied for the inn at Killin in 1807. [NRS.GD112.11.8.1.14]

CAMPBELL, PETER, from Killin, emigrated on the Harmony bound for Canada in 1817, settled in Glovesville, Ontario. [CGS.274]

CAMPBELL, ROBERT, a farmer at Balloleys, Abernyte, a victim of theft in 1826. [NRS.AD14.26.48]

CAMPBELL, WALTER, born 1745, Captain of the Prince of Wales' American Regiment of Foot, died in Perth on 18 May 1823, husband of Nancy de Weber, born 1774, died in Dunkeld on 9 September 1828. [Perth, Greyfriars, gravestone]

CAMPBELL, WILLIAM, probably from Crieff, a mason in Hanover County, Jamaica, a will dated 1807. [NRS.RD3.318.349]

CAMPBELL, WILLIAM, a woodcutter at Callagant, Aberfoyle, was accused of homicide in 1820. [NRS.AD14.20.252]

CAMPBELL, WILLIAM, born 1825, son of Peter Campbell, a dyer in Perth, and his wife Margaret McKechnie, died in Sydney, New South Wales, Australia, on 17 February 1860. [Greyfriars gravestone, Perth]

CANTWELL, Mrs ANNIE, born 1788 in Crannich, Weem, died in 1850, wife of Michael Cantwell. [Wallace gravestone, Cumberland County, Nova Scotia]

CAREHAR, JANET, born 1779, a thief who was sentenced to transportation to the colonies, at Perth on 17 September 1833. [PKA.B59.26.11]

CARGILL, JAMES STEWART, a Lieutenant on half pay of the 52$^{nd}$ Regiment of Foot, in Dunkeld, was accused of assault in 1822. [NRS.AD14.22.109]; also, in 1824. [NRS.AD14.24.73]

CARMICHAEL, ALEXANDER, in Baillie Ross's Close, High Street, Perth, was accused of house-breaking and theft in 1825. [NRS.JC26.1825.295]

CARMICHAEL, ANN, in Meal Vennel, Perth, a victim of theft in 1830. [NRS.AD14.30.21]

CARMICHAEL, DUNCAN, at Bridge of Lochtay, Killin, lately returned from the West Indies, son of Peter Carmichael a wood keeper, a petition, 1807. [NRS.GD112.11.8.1.21]

CARMICHAEL, JOHN, with his wife Ann, from Comrie, emigrated via Greenock aboard the Curlew bound for Quebec on 21 July 1818. [TNA.CO384/3.123-127]

CARMICHAEL, JOHN, a labourer in Wester Aberfeldy, was accused of theft in 1833. [NRS.AD14.33.86]

CARMICHAEL, LAWRENCE, son of Robert Carmichael, [1771-1832], and his wife Janet Dougall, [1772-1840], died in America. [Milnathort gravestone, Kinross]

CARMICHAEL, PETER, from Perthshire, died on Whitehall Estate, Jamaica, in 1802. [EEC.142241]

CARNABY, WILLIAM, born 1806 in Perth, a Justice in Claredon, Jamaica, died on 18 March 1841. [Old Harbour gravestone, Jamaica]

CARNEGIE, PATRICK, a messenger in Coupar Angus, 1801. [NRS.GD16.41.1007]

CAW, JAMES, a farmer in Pitmurthly with land in Madderty in 1807. [NRS.GD155.304]

CAW,....., son of Thomas Caw the Customs Collector, was born in Perth on 24 June 1820. [SM.86.94]

CHALMERS, ANNE, wife of James Moncur in Hatton of Rattray, sister of Gilbert Chalmers deceased, a decreet, 1809. [NRS.GD83.897]

CHALMERS, DAVID, in Alyth, brother of Gilbert Chalmers deceased, a decreet, 1809. [NRS.GD83.897]

CHALMERS, GEORGE, born 1825, son of John Chalmers and his wife Elizabeth Geddes, died in Havanna, Cuba, on 5 June 1862. [Bendochy gravestone]

CHALMERS, HELEN, in Hatton of Rattray, sister of Gilbert Chalmers deceased, a decreet, 1809. [NRS.GD83.897]

CHALMERS, MARY, wife of James Ogilvy in Alyth, sister of Gilbert Chalmers deceased, a decreet, 1809. [NRS.GD83.897]

CHALMERS, PETER, born 1844, son of Peter Chalmers and his wife Helen Spence, died in San Antonio, Texas, on 26 April 1879. [Dron gravestone]

CHAPMAN, GEORGE BROWN, born 1808, son of Laurence Chapman, [1783-1839], and his wife Isobel Brown, [1773-1862], died on St

Vincent, British West Indies, on 25 August 1839. [Blairgowrie gravestone]

CHAPMAN, JAMES, son of Robert Chapman, [1795-1880], and his wife Mary Ramsay Duncan, [1810-1880], settled in Brisbane, Queensland, Australia. [Dunbarney gravestone]

CHRISTIE, ALEXANDER, a carter, guilty of forgery, was sentenced to transportation to the colonies for life, at Perth in September 1834. [PKA.B59.26.11.3.6]

CHRISTIE, DONALD, [1], probably from Perthshire, settled in Reach, Canada West, by 1848. [NRS.GD112.61.5/2]

CHRISTIE, DONALD, [2], probably from Perthshire, settled in Reach, Canada West, by 1848. [NRS.GD112.61.5/2]

CHRISTIE, DONALD, [3], probably from Perthshire, settled in Reach, Canada West, by 1848. [NRS.GD112.61.5/2]

CHRISTIE, DUNCAN, [1], probably from Perthshire, settled in Reach, Canada West, by 1848. [NRS.GD112.61.5/2]

CHRISTIE, DUNCAN,[2], probably from Perthshire, settled in Reach, Canada West, by 1848. [NRS.GD112.61.5/2]

CHRISTIE, JOHN, born 1745, married Janet McGregor, [1757-1852], from Killin, settled at Creek Road, Mumford, New York, in 1797, died on 3 July 1843.

CHRISTIE, JOHN, [1], probably from Perthshire, settled in Reach, Canada West, by 1848. [NRS.GD112.61.5/2]

CHRISTIE, JOHN, [2], probably from Perthshire, settled in Reach, Canada West, by 1848. [NRS.GD112.61.5/2]

CHRISTIE, JOHN, [3], probably from Perthshire, settled in Reach, Canada West, by 1848. [NRS.GD112.61.5/2]

CHRISTIE, MALCOLM, in Glen Dochart, Killin, a victim of cattle theft in 1837. [NRS.AD14.37.528]

CHRISTIE, PETER, probably from Perthshire, settled in Reach, Canada West, by 1848. [NRS.GD112.61.5/2]

CHRISTIE, ROBERT, a labourer in Scotlandwell, Kinross, was accused of assault and poaching in 1830. [NRS.AD14.30.8]

CLARK, ALEXANDER, with his wife Janet and one child from Comrie, emigrated via Greenock aboard the Curlew bound for Quebec on 21 July 1818. [TNA.CO384/3.123-127]

CLARK, ALEXANDER, an innkeeper in Waterloo, Auchtergaven, was charged with an assault with a firearm in 1831. [NRS.AD14.31.59]

CLARK, DONALD, with his wife Margaret, from Comrie, emigrated via Greenock aboard the Curlew bound for Quebec on 21 July 1818. [TNA.CO384/3.123-127]

CLARKE, DUNCAN, a wheelwright in Killin, a petition, 1805. [NRS.GD112.11.7.8.5]

CLARK or KERR, ELIZABETH, born 1778, a widow, guilty of theft, was sentenced to be transported to the colonies for seven years, at Perth in October 1832. [PKA.B59.26.11.3.6]

CLARK, JAMES, a shoemaker in Pitcairngreen, Redgorton, was accused of theft in 1832. [NRS.AD14.32.28]

CLARK, JEAN, wife of Peter Gowans in Crieff, dead by 1829, mother of John Gowans in Tennessee. [NRS.S/H]

CLARK, JOHN, a surgeon in Dunkeld, later in London, letters to Colonel Alan McPherson of Blairgowrie, from 1799 to 1812. [NRS.GD80.941]

CLARK, JOHN, son of Frederick Clark and his wife Elizabeth Kidd in Coupar Angus, died in St Mary's, Jamaica, on 15 May 1833, [Coupar Angus gravestone]

CLARK, JOHN, from Perth, settled in Australia by 1859. [NRS.S/H]

CLARK, LAWRENCE, in Auchterarder, died in April 1829. [NRS.S/H.1878]

CLARK, MARY, daughter of Ewan Clark a gardener at Lawton, Cargill, versus John Stewart a jailer in Forfar, a process of divorce in 1828. [NRS.CC8.6.2105]

CLARK, PETER, a writer in Coupar Angus, versus James Anderson a blacksmith and feuar in Coupar Angus, 1822. [NRS.CS44.10.29]

CLARKE, Reverend WILLIAM C., rector of Elizabethtown, Toronto, Ontario, second son of Robert Clarke of Comrie Castle, married Ann Charity Pigot, eldest daughter of William D. Pigot of Dysart, Queen's County, Ireland, at Fitzroy Castle, Canada West, on 15 June 1856. [W]

CLEMENT, JOHN, a weaver at Smiddyhaugh, Auchterarder, trial papers, 1813. [NRS.JC26.1813.15]

CLOW, DAVID, born 1836, son of Richard Clow and his wife Ann Barclay, died in Colorado on 1 January 1882. [Dunning gravestone]

COLDSTREAM, JOHN, the Commissary Clerk of Dunblane, versus Sarah Shearer, in 1821. [NRS.CS36.31.87]

COMRIE, PETER, with his wife Jane and two children, from Comrie, emigrated via Greenock aboard the Curlew bound for Quebec on 21 July 1818. [TNA.CO384/3.123-127]

COMRIE, PETER, an innkeeper in Comrie, died 13 April 1855, father of James Comrie in Cincinatti. [NRS.S/H.1855]

CONACHER, ALEXANDER, born 1846, son of David Conacher and his wife Helen Stewart, died in USA on 10 September 1897. [Moulin gravestone]

CONNACHER, DAVID, a tanner in Dunkeld, sequestration, 1830. [NRS.CS236.C9.12]

CONNACHER, DONALD, in Tomintianda, accused of assault in 1810. [NRS.JC26.1810.3]

CONNACHER, JAMES, a linen manufacturer in Dunkeld, previously the stamp master of Blairgowrie, 1827. [NRS.NG1.64.41]

CONNACHER, PETER, a merchant in Dunkeld, deceased, a decreet, 1815. [NRS.CS36.13.51]

CONNAL, DANIEL, a farmer and grain dealer in Blackford in 1850. [NRS.CS280.36.29]

CONNAL, JOHN, and DAVID CONNAL, manufacturers in Blackford, 1850. [NRS.CS280.36.30]

CONSTABLE, DAVID, of High Street, Blairgowrie, victim of assault in 1831. [NRS.JC26.1831.211]

CONSTABLE, GEORGE, in the West Mains of Castle Huntly, Longforgan, a victim of arson in 1844. [NRS.AD14.44.27]

CONSTABLE, WILLIAM, alias JAMES RAMSAY, farmer in Bendochy, accused of forgery in 1830. [NRS.AD14.30.100]

COOK, DAVID, born 1819 in Kinross, accused of theft in Edinburgh in 1831. [NRS.AD14.31.464]

COOKE, JANET, daughter of John Cooke a merchant in Crieff, married Patrick McDougall from Grenada, in Crieff on 24 November 1818. [S.98.18]. Patrick McDougall died in St George, Grenada, on 25 July 1829. [BM.26.842]

COOK, ROBERT, found guilty of theft at West Burn, Auchterarder and sentenced to transportation to the colonies for seven years in 1836. [NRS.JC36.1836.139]

CORNFUTE, JAMES, son of George Cornfute a merchant in Perth, a student at Marshal College, Aberdeen, in 1835. [MCA]

COUPAR, JOHN, an apprentice mason at Lochrin Moss, Kinross, was accused of assault and stabbing in 1832. [NRS.AD14.32.189]

COUTTS, DAVID, from Logiealmond, a divinity student in 1823, later a minister in Canada. [UPC]

COWAN, DAVID, born 1830, son of William Cowan, [1807-1889], and his wife Julia Sim, [1799-1875], a merchant in Toronto, Ontario, died 13 January 1882 in Winnipeg, Manitoba, buried at Mount Pleasant, Toronto. [Rattray gravestone]

COWAN, DAVID, born 1837, son of John Cowan and his wife Janet Mill, died in St Francis, Quebec, Canada, on 3 November 1875. [Dunbarney gravestone]

COWAN, HUGH, a weaver, was accused of using counterfeit coins at Allen's Arms Inn in Errol in 1837. [NRS.AD14.37.99]

COWAN, MARY, born 1837, daughter of William Cowan and his wife Julia Sim, wife of John Hillock in Toronto, Ontario, Canada, died on 23 February 1896, buried at Mount Pleasant, Toronto, Ontario. [Rattray gravestone]

CRAIG, WILLIAM, born 1822, from Kinnoull, died in New York on 15 January 1873. [EC.27558]

CRAM, JOHN, with his wife Isabella and one child, from Comrie, emigrated via Greenock aboard the <u>Curlew</u> bound for Quebec on 21 July 1818. [TNA.CO384/3.123-127]

CRAWFORD, ROBERT, in Dunblane, 1818, a partner in the Allan Flax Spinning Company. [NRS.CS96.3561]; a merchant in Dunblane, was accused of assault in 1819. [NRS.AD14.19.220]

CRAWFORD, ROBERT, born 1807, a labourer, accused of the culpable homicide of his mother Margaret Crawford in Dunblane in 1835. [NRS.AD14.35.142]

CREE, ALEXANDER, of the Honourable East India Company Service, son of James Cree in Perth, testament, 1792, Comm. Edinburgh. [NRS]

CREIGHTON, WILLIAM, in Burndale, Bendochy, accused of bigamy in 1832. [NRS.AD14.32.120]

CRERAR, or MCINTOSH, ANDREW, a labourer in Wester Aberfeldy, accused of theft in 1833. [NRS.AD14.33.86]

CRERAR, JANET, a tenant in Murthly, petitioned for her son Donald, found guilty of beating an Excise officer, then whipped through the streets of Perth before being taken to the hulks at Woolwich, being transported to the colonies for fourteen years, in 1825. [NRS.GD112.11.9.1.4; JC26.1825.16]

CRERAR, JOHN, tenant at Lochbuy, Ardtalanaig, was brought before the Excise Court accused of having an illegal whisky still in 1822. [NRS.GD112.11.8.14.2]

CRERAR, JOHN, a boatman in Perth, dead by 1852, father of John Crerar a baker in New York. [NRS.S/H]

CRICHTON, JAMES, a shoemaker in Coupar Angus, son of Robert Crichton in Causewayend, Coupar Angus, accused of theft in 1818. [NRS.AD14.18.178]

CRICHTON, JOHN, a shoemaker in Coupar Angus, son of Robert Crichton in Causewayend, Coupar Angus, accused of theft in 1818. [NRS.AD14.18.178]

CROSBIE, MARTHA, or MARGARET, born 1789, widow of Reverend William Dunn in Coupar Angus, died in Melbourne, Victoria, Australia, on 5 December 1852. [Coupar Angus gravestone]

CROWN, THOMAS, from Perth, an Admiral of the Royal Navy, later an Admiral of the Russian Navy, died in St Petersburg, Russia, in 1841. [Mariners of Dundee, 2006, 149]

CRUICKSHANK, JOHN, born 1766, late in St Vincent, died in Coupar Angus on 29 July 1810. [EA.4863.87]

CULBERT, JANET, born 1772, wife of Robert Whyte a merchant, died in Perth on 17 November 1825. [SM.97.127]

CUPPLES, GEORGE, minister in Kilmadock, a petition, 1845. [NRS.GD112.51.189]

DALGLEISH, ADAM, 1794-1855, and his wife Martha Camron, 1808-1858, parents of Catherine Craig Dalgleish in San Francisco, California. [Tulliallan gravestone]

DALLAS, CHRISTINE, with a thread mill at Bridgend of Perth, a petition, 1803. [PKA.B59.24.8.35]

DARLING, JOSEPH, a burglar who was sentenced to be transported to the colonies for seven years, at Perth in April 1832. [PKA.B59.26.11.3.6]

DAVIDSON, JOHN, carter in Muthill, was accused of assault in Glendevon in 1822. [NRS.A14.22.58]

DAVIDSON, LAWRENCE, a shoemaker in Methven, was accused of assault in 1831. [NRS.AD14.]

DAVIDSON, ROBERT, in Auchterarder, a petition for an interest in the Royal Mail coach between Glasgow and Perth in 1833. [NRS.GD112.11.10.14]

DAVIDSON, THOMAS, in Drumlochie, Blackford, a victim of horse theft in 1831. [NRS.AD14.31.2]

DEAN, ALEXANDER, in Duncreavy, Arngask, a victim of assault in 1837. [NRS.AD14.37.164]

DEMPSTER, BEATRIX, wife of John Gardiner late tenant in Pitkeathly Wells, died in Charleton, New York, in 1807. [DPCA.262]

DEMPSTER, DAVID, late of Gettysburg, York County, Pennsylvania, later in Wester Taliochie, Kinross, in 1800. [NRS.CS18.712.24]

DEMPSTER, WILLIAM, from Tillyochie, Kinross, settled in London, Ontario, before 1876. [EC.28606]

DEUCHARS, JAMES, in Kepp, Dunblane, was accused of hamesucken in 1825. [NRS.AD14.25.248]

DEUCHARS, JOHN, jr., a shoemaker in Middle Benchillis accused of assault in 1810. [NRS.JC26.1810.3]

DEUCHARS, THOMAS, son of John Deuchars a woolspinner in Perth, was apprenticed to David Young a coppersmith in Perth, for four and a half years in 1808. [NRS.GD1.467.16/10]

DEWAR, ARCHIBALD, with his wife Margaret and two children, from Comrie, emigrated via Greenock aboard the Curlew bound for Quebec on 21 July 1818. [TNA.CO384/3.123-127]

DEWAR, ARCHIBALD, in New Breadalbane, Canada, in 1823, brother of Donald Dewar in Ardonag. [NRS.RH1.2.539/1]

DEWAR, COLIN, born 1792, a labourer from Kenmore, emigrated via Port Glasgow aboard the Favourite of St John bound for St John, New Brunswick, on 22 October 1815. [PANB.ms.RS23E.fo.9798]

DEWAR, DONALD, born 1786, a labourer from Foss, with his wife Margaret born 1788, emigrated aboard the Clarendon of Hull bound for Prince Edward Island in August 1808. [NSARM] [TNA.CO226.23]

DEWAR, DUNCAN, an innkeeper in Birnam, was murdered in 1832. [NRS.AD14.32.6]

DEWAR, JAMES, in Duntuim, petitioned for a house in Aberfeldy in 1808. [NRS.GD112.11.8.4.15]

DEWAR, JOHN, born 1786, a labourer from Kenmore, emigrated via Port Glasgow aboard the Favourite of St John bound for St John, New Brunswick, on 22 October 1815. [PANB.ms.RS23E.fo.9798]

DEWAR, JOHN, from Comrie, emigrated via Greenock aboard the Curlew bound for Quebec on 21 July 1818. [TNA.CO384/3.123-127]

DEWAR, JOHN, from Dull, with his wife Emily Knight, and son John born 22 August 1829, emigrated to Canada in 1829, settled in Esquessing, Halton County, Ontario. [TVFHS]

DEWAR, MALCOLM, with his wife Ann and two children, from Comrie, emigrated via Greenock aboard the Curlew bound for Quebec on 21 July 1818. [TNA.CO384/3.123-127]

DEWAR, MARGARET, widow of John Robertson a miller in Aberfeldy, a petition, 1803. [NRS.GD112.11.7.6.13]

DEWAR, PETER, born 1759, a farmer from Kenmore, with his wife Betsy born 1765, and children Jean born 1795, a servant, John born 1794 a labourer, Margaret born 1796 a servant, Janet born 1795 a servant, Hugh born 1799, and James born 1785 a labourer, emigrated via Port Glasgow aboard the Favourite of St John bound for St John, New Brunswick, on 22 October 1815. [PANB.ms.RS23E.fo.9798]

DEWAR, PETER, from Comrie, emigrated via Greenock aboard the Curlew bound for Quebec on 21 July 1818. [TNA.CO384/3.123-127]

DEWAR, PETER, born 1812, son of Donald Dewar in Qupig, [1760-1826] and his wife Helen Murray, [1776-1839], died in America in February 1837. [Moonzievaird gravestone]

DEWAR, PETER, in Aberfeldy, deceased, a sequestration petition in 1848. [NRS.CS228.1.22]

DEWAR, THOMAS, born 1748 in Perthshire, emigrated with his wife E.O. Dempster, via Greenock bound for New York aboard the Recovery on 4 August 1808. [NLS.ms.*1053]*

DICK, JAMES CHARLES, born 23 August 1792, fourth son of Dr Dick of Tullymet, died on 17 November 1831. [Bareilly gravestone, Bengal]

DICK, JAMES, a general merchant in Blairgowrie, 1800. [NRS.GD257.23.44]

DICK, WILLIAM, born 1868, son of William Dick and his wife Christina Robb, died in Ansonia, Connecticut on 27 October 1889. [Longforgan gravestone]

DICKIE, ROBERT, in Gallowridge, father of Betsy Anderson Dickie who married Robert Garrow, at 182 Seventh Avenue, New York, on 17 September 1869. [S.8170]

DICKSON, CHARLES RANALDSON, second son of David R. Dickson of Blairhall, married Fanny Macartney, daughter of J. Macartney a banker in Carlow, in Hamilton, Upper Canada, on 7 January 1843. [AJ.4965][EEC.20554]

DONALD, DAVID, a merchant in Rattray, versus James Ewing a grocer in Perth, 1813. [NRS.CS40.14.15]

DONALD, JAMES, born 1822, son of David Donald and his wife Elizabeth Whitehead, died at Partook off the Mosquito Coast, Nicaragua, on 27 August 1852. [Kinnoull gravestone]

DONALDSON, DAVID, jr., a baker in Coupar Angus, eldest son of David Donaldson in Cupar, Fife, a decreet, 1815. [NRS.CS42.14.33]

DONALDSON, DUNCAN, born 1794, a labourer from Killin, emigrated via Port Glasgow aboard the Favourite of St John bound for St John, New Brunswick, on 22 October 1815. [PANB.ms.RS23E.fo.9798]

DONALDSON, WILLIAM, born 1852 in Milnathort, a merchant in Minneapolis, died in California on 30 January 1899. [S.17351]

DOUGLAS, ALEXANDER, with his wife Elizabeth, from Dull, emigrated via Greenock aboard the Curlew bound for Quebec on 21 July 1818. [TNA.CO384/3.123-127]

DOUGLAS, DANIEL, born 1785, a labourer from Craganfearn, Logerait, emigrated via Greenock aboard the William of New York bound for New York on 4 September 1817, landed there on 17 October 1817. [NY Municipal Archives] [NY Commercial Advertiser, 18.10.1817]

DOUGLAS, DAVID, born 1798 in Scone, a botanist in California, Oregon, and Washington, from 1823 to 1832, died in the Sandwich Islands, [Hawaii], in 1834. [New Scone gravestone]

DOUGLAS, JOHN, born 1840, son of William Douglas, a messenger-at-arms in Perth, and his wife Jane, died in Stratford, Ontario, on 4 May 1864. [Perth, Greyfriars, gravestone]

DOUGLAS, TOM, born 1850 in Perth, died in 1906. [Blewett Pass gravestone, Chelan County, Washington]

DOW, GEORGE, born 1861, son of Alexander Dow and his wife Margaret Donaldson, died 1912 in Edmonton, Canada. [Methven gravestone]

DOW, JOHN, born 1792, an apprentice surgeon from Perth, emigrated via Greenock aboard the Pitt bound for New York on 14 September 1803. [NLS.ms1053]

DOW, PATRICK, a dyke builder in Strowan, 1803. [NRS.GD132.687]

DOW, SARAH, daughter of John Dow a dyer in Dunning, versus William Edie a maltman in Dunning, 18.. [NRS.CC8.6.1551]

DOW, WILLIAM, son of Dr William Dow, [1765-1844], and his wife Anne Mason, settled in Montreal, Quebec. [Muthill gravestone]

DOW, WILLIAM, son of Reverend Dow in Blairgowrie, died in Antigua on 7 July 1803. [EEC.14316]

DOW,..., stamp-master in Blairgowrie, letters, 1816. [NRS.GD385.67]

DOWNIE, JOHN, in Colden, Kinross, a victim of assault and stabbing in 1832. [NRS.AD14.32.189]

DREW, THOMAS, was found guilty of theft and fraud in Perth and Kinross, was sentenced to transportation to the colonies for seven years, on 22 August 1846. [NRS.JC26.1847.637]

DRON, ALEXANDER, in Drum of Garvock, Dunning, a victim of housebreaking in 1836. [NRS.AD14.36.77]

DRON, GEORGE, in James Murray's Royal Asylum for Lunatics in Perth, son of William Dron of Aberuthven, 1844. [NRS.CS313.36]

DRON, JOHN, a coal merchant in Perth, 1841. [NRS.CS280.27.22]

DRON, MARY, daughter of James Dron in Abernethy, a victim of crime in 1823. [NRS.JC26.1823.198]

DRON, WILLIAM, a bookseller in Auchterarder, father of John Dron who died in Cape Town, South Africa, on 4 July 1884. [S.12822]

DRUMMOND, DAVID, a surgeon, son of John Drummond a baker in Crieff, settled in Sydney, New South Wales, by 1848. [NRS.S/H]

DRUMMOND, FRANCIS, master of the Jean of Perth in 1796. [NRS.CE70.1.14]

DRUMMOND, GAVIN, born 1812, a wright in Auchterarder, was accused of poaching in 1835. [NRS.AD14.35.100]

DRUMMOND, JAMES, master of the Antelope of Perth in 1795. [NRS.CE70.1.8/58]; testament, 1798. [NRS.CC3]

DRUMMOND, JAMES, born 1788 in Perthshire, a Superintendent of the Swan River Colony, Western Australia, in 1830, with his wife Sarah born 1790, and children Thomas, Jane, James, John N., Johnston, and Euphemia, all born in Perthshire. [BPP.3.436]

DRUMMOND, JAMES, in New York, died there on 21 February 1801, probably from Perthshire, testament, 1806, Comm. Edinburgh. [NRS]

DRUMMOND, JAMES, born 1790, a labourer from Quoig, Comrie, emigrated via Greenock aboard the William of New York bound for New York on 4 September 1817, landed there on 17 October 1817. [NY Municipal Archives] [NY Commercial Advertiser, 18.10.1817]

DRUMMOND, JAMES, in Aberuchill, Comrie, a letter, 1833. [NRS.GD112.74.39.53]

DRUMMOND, JOHN, born 1773, a labourer from Methven, emigrated via Greenock aboard the Pitt bound for New York on 14 September 1803. [NLS.ms1053]

DRUMMOND, JOHN, born 1815, a wright in Auchterarder, was accused of poaching in 1835. [NRS.AD14.35.100]

DRUMMOND, Reverend JOHN STEWART, born 1852, minister at Yarra Glen Church, Victoria, Australia, died in September 1918. [Gask gravestone]

DRUMMOND, MALCOLM, with his wife Christine and two children, from Comrie, emigrated via Greenock aboard the Curlew bound for Quebec on 21 July 1818. [TNA.CO384/3.123-127]

DRUMMOND, ROBERT, a lime and corn merchant in Perth, business correspondence, 1812. [PKA.B59.37.3.2]

DRUMMOND, THOMAS, from Perthshire, a botanist in Texas from 1833 until 1835, died in Havanna, Cuba.

DRUMMOND, WILLIAM, was found guilty of housebreaking and was sentenced in Perth in 1814 to be transported to the colonies for life. [NRS.GD1.959]

DRUMMOND, WILLIAM, a weaver in Dunning, was accused of theft in 1818. [NRS.AD14.18.31]

DRYSDALE, JOHN, a manservant in Hawkhill, Kinross, was accused of arson in 1830. [NRS.AD14.30.356]

DRYSDALE, THOMAS, in Milnathort, Kinross, a bond of caution, 1803. [NRS.271.581]

DUCAT, Dr ALEXANDER, from Perthshire, died at Bunker's Hill, Jamaica, on 8 September 1807. [SM.69.958]

DUFF, ALEXANDER, from Nether Kincarnie, emigrated via Liverpool bound for North America in June 1833. [SG.2.152]

DUFF, ALEXANDER, born 1773, a labourer from Methven, emigrated via Greenock aboard the Pitt bound for New York on 14 September 1803. [NLS.ms1053]

DUFF, Mrs BARBARA, born 1789 in Perthshire, emigrated to New Brunswick with her husband Charles Duff in 1801, died in St Mary's, Nashwaak, on 8 April 1836. [New Brunswick Royal Gazette, 13.4.1836]

DUFF, CHARLES, born 5 June 1770 at Mains of Kinnaird, son of Charles Duff and his wife Isobel Robertson, settled in New Brunswick around 1801, died in Fredericton, N.B., on 20 February 1829. [NBC. 7 March 1829]

DUFF, DONALD, servant to James Duff a tenant in Letha, Moneydie, accused of assault in 1810. NRS.JC26.1810.3]

DUFF, HARRIET REID, daughter of John Duff, [1803-1890], settled in Montreal, Quebec. [Cargill gravestone]

DUFF, JAMES, from Abernethy, died in New York State before March 1815. [NRS.CS17.1.34/317]

DUFF, JAMES, from Kindallachan, emigrated via Liverpool bound for North America in June 1833. [SG.2.152]

DUFF, JAMES, a merchant in Perth, trading with Archangel, Russia, between 1846 and 1848. [NRS.CS96.53]

DUFF, JOHN, a merchant in Dunkeld an inventory of title deeds, 1823. [PKA.B59.40.270]

DUFF, JOHN, from Kindallachan, emigrated via Liverpool bound for North America in June 1833. [SG.2.152]

DUFF, THOMAS, from Kindallachan, emigrated via Liverpool bound for North America in June 1833. [SG.2.152]

DUFFUS, ELIZABETH, born 1807, wife of James Pringle a farmer of Graymond, Bendochy, was accused of theft and destroying a trust disposition in Forfar 1848. [NRS.AC14.48.421]

DUFFUS, ELSPETH, wife of William Duffus in New Rattray, victim of assault at Causewayend Road, Perth, in 1848. [AD14.48.473]

DUFFUS, EUPHEMIA, born 1803, in Errachtbank, Rattray, was accused of theft and destroying a trust disposition in Forfar 1848. [NRS.AC14.48.421]

DUFFUS, JANE, born 1808, in Erracht Bank, Rattray, was accused of theft and destroying a trust disposition in Forfar 1848. [NRS.AC14.48.421]

DUFFUS, or WYLLIE, JANE, from Erichtbank, Blairgowrie, later in Airleywight, Washington, New York, a sasine, 28 February 1849. [NRS.RS.Forfar.16.18]

DUFFUS, MARGARET, born 1798, wife of John Rattray in Coralbank, Rattray, was accused of theft and destroying a trust disposition in Forfar 1848. [NRS.AC14.48.421]

DUNCAN, JAMES, [1736-1786], a wright in Perth, and his wife Anne Simpson, [1747-1829], parents of John Duncan who died in Charleston, South Carolina. [Greyfriars gravestone, Perth]

DUNCAN, JAMES, born 1827 in Alyth, a merchant in Dundee and New York, died at Jordanstone, Alyth, on 29 January 1909. [ANY]

DUNCAN, JOHN, son of John Duncan, [1736-1786], a wright in Perth, and his wife Ann Simpson, [1747-1829], died in Charleston, South Carolina. [Perth, Greyfriars, gravestone]

DUNCAN, JOHN, son of John Duncan a tacksman, in Pottie Mill, Dron, was accused of forgery in 1816. [NRS.AD14.16.30]

DUNCAN, JOHN, born 1790 in Perthshire, his wife Jane born 1786 in Dundee, their children Ann born 1816 in Fife, Ellen born 1818 in Fife, David born 1820 in Fife, and daughter Jane born 1822 in New York city, he settled in New York as a merchant in 1821, they were naturalised there on 20 February 1823. [N.Y. Court of Common Pleas Records]

DUNCAN, PETER, guilty of assault, was sentenced to transportation to the colonies for seven years, at Perth in 1829. [PKA.B59.26.11.3]

DUNCAN, SUSAN, daughter of Alexander Duncan in Essie, versus Alexander Watt a merchant in Coupar Angus, now a butcher in Arbroath, a process of separation, 1808. [NRS.CC8.6.1306]

DUNCAN, WILLIAM, born 1828, son of James Duncan and his wife Isabel Craig, died in Melbourne, Victoria, Australia, on 27 October 1861. [Perth Greyfriars gravestone]

DUNCAN, WILLIAM, born in 1850, son of David Duncan and his wife Elizabeth Crockatt, died in Sydney, New South Wales, Australia, on 5 February 1889, [Collace gravestone]

DUNCANSON, GEORGE, died in Port Adelaide, South Australia, on 29 June 1859. [Perth Greyfriars gravestone]

DUNCANSON, JAMES, from Dunblane, a labourer in Stirling, was accused of theft in 1819. [NRS.AD14.19.241]

DUNCANSON, ROBERT, born 1787, a labourer from Callendar, emigrated via Port Glasgow aboard the <u>Favourite of St John</u> bound for St John, New Brunswick, on 22 October 1815. [PANB.ms.RS23E.fo.9798]

DUNCANSON, ROBERT, apprentice mason in Doune, Kilmadock, accused of hamesucken, assault, and theft in 1818. [NRS.AD14.18.88]

DUNDAS, WILLIAM, of Ochtertyre, late in the Service of the Honourable East India Company in Bengal, died at Niagara Falls on 20 August 1842. [EEC.20509]

DUNN, ALEXANDER, in Keithock Mills, Coupar Angus, a sequestration petition in 1843. [NRS.CS278.2/5]

EADIE, ANDREW, son of Robert Eadie [1760-1837] in Dunblane, emigrated to Canada between 1815 and 1820. [SG]

EADIE, JOHN, born 1803, a weaver in Dunblane, son of Helen Eadie, was accused of administering drugs, in 1822. [NRS.AD14.22.105]

EADIE, JOHN, a farmer, cattle dealer, and maltster in Stonehill, Dunblane, sederunt book, 1827-1828. [NRS.CS96.2055]

EADIE, ROBERT, son of John Eadie a weaver at Bridge-end of Dunblane, was accused of hamesucken and assault in 1830. [NRS.AD14.31.20]

EADIE, THOMAS, born 1809, a weaver in Dunblane, was accused of bigamy in 1831, being married to Jean .... In Dunblane, later to Margaret Morrison in Glasgow. [NRS.AD14.43.291]

EADIE, ANDREW, son of Robert Eadie [1760-1837] in Dunblane, emigrated to Canada between 1815 and 1820. [SG]

EASON, JAMES, trustee of William McLaren in Wester Rhynd, versus Thomas Glass and his wife Ann McLaren, a decreet, 1816. [NRS.CS40.21.111]

EASSON, ROBERT, son of Andrew Easson a farm servant at Pitkindie, Abernyte, was accused of homicide in 1836. [NRS.AD14.36.451]

EASTON, JAMES GARDINER, born 1820, son of John Easton and his wife Martha Gardiner, died in Valparaiso, Chile, on 19 August 1847. [Luncarty gravestone]

EDWARDS, ALEXANDER, and WILLIAM, cattle dealers at Crathies Boat, Meigle, sederunt book, 1807-1808. [NRS.CS96.678]

ELDER, ALEXANDER, born 27 June 1804 in Milnathort, Kinross, son of William Elder and his wife Christiana Mailer, was educated at Glasgow University in 1830, a physician who settled in New York, died in New Jersey on 3 February 1875. [ANY]

ELDER, JOHN, a wright and feuar in Blairgowrie, dead by 1789, father of Peter Elder at Seven Rivers, Jamaica. [NRS.S/H]

ELDER, WILLIAM, a wright in Perth, a testament, 1798, Comm. St Andrews. [NRS]

ELDER, WILLIAM, and his wife Christiana Mailer, in Milnathort, Kinross, emigrated to New York in 1828, settled at West Farms, Schenectady County, N.Y. [ANY]

ENVERDALE, DAVID, in Blairgowrie and Dunkeld, a sequestration petition, 1843. [NRS.CS279.665]

ENVERDALE, DAVID KERR, son of David Enverdale a merchant in Coupar Angus, a student at Marischal College, Aberdeen, in 1840s, later a teacher in Southsea. [MCA]

FAICHNEY, ANN, from Perth, wife of John Blair, died in South Carolina, testament, 1797, Comm. Edinburgh. [NRS]

FAICHNEY, ELIZABETH, in Perth, testament, 1797, Comm. St Andrews. [NRS]

FAICHNEY, GEORGE, Provost of Perth, testament, 1792, Comm. St Andrews. [NRS]

FAICHNEY, THOMAS, a merchant in Perth, testament, 1792, Comm. St Andrews. [NRS]

FAIRLEY, CORNELIUS, in Meal Vennel, Perth, a victim of theft in 1832. [NRS.AD14.29.129]

FAIRNIE, DAVID, a linen manufacturer in Perth, testament, 1790, Comm. St Andrews. [NRS]

FARQUHARSON, DAVID, a tenant in Rochallie, Blairgowrie, testament, 1800, Comm. St Andrews. [NRS]

FARQUHARSON, DAVID, and his wife Ann Potter, in Perth Tolbooth was accused of forgery in 1827. [NRS.JC26.1827.392]

FARQUHARSON, THOMAS, in Perthshire, factor of James Lindsay in St Thomas in the East, Jamaica, a deed in 1806. [NRS.RD3.315.571]

FENTON, GEORGE, born 1811, son of James Fenton a fisherman, Blairgowrie, was accused of housebreaking in 1827. [NRS.AD14.27.197]

FENTON, ROBERT, a butcher in Perth, guilty of stealing sheep, was sentenced to transportation to the colonies for seven years, at Perth on 23 April 1812. [Scots Magazine.84.391]

FENWICK, JOHN, in Milnathort, a victim of rioting in Dollar in 1837. [NRS.AD14.37.475]

FENWICK, WILLIAM, jr., in Milnathort, Kinross, a victim of rioting in Dollar in 1837. [NRS.AD14.37.475]

FERGUSON, ADAM, an advocate, from Woodhill, Perthshire, a member of the Legislative Council of Canada, died in Woodhill, Canada East, on 25 September 1862. [S.2284][AJ.5988] [W.XXIII.2498][GM.NS2/13.788]

FERGUSON, AGNES, widow of James Scott Ferguson fifth son of Adam Ferguson of Woodhill, died in Gamonoque, Canada West, on 13 March 1852. [W.XIII.1319]

FERGUSON, ALEXANDER EDMUND, born 1801, son of Alexander Ferguson of Baledmond, died on St Iago Estate, Clarendon, Jamaica, on 6 June 1831. [AJ.4366]

FERGUSON, ALEXANDER, youngest son of James Ferguson in Thornhill, Muthill, a merchant in New Braufels, Texas, died there on 4 March 1860. [S.1497]

FERGUSON, ARCHIBALD, a messenger in Dunblane, having seized a cartload of illicit whisky was assaulted in 1803. [NRS.JC26.1803.6]

FERGUSON, ARCHIBALD, born 1795, a labourer from Callendar, emigrated via Port Glasgow aboard the Favourite of St John bound for St John, New Brunswick, on 22 October 1815. [PANB.ms.RS23E.fo.9798]

FERGUSON, CATHERINE, sewing mistress in Aberfeldy for thirteen years, applied for the house occupied by Mrs McNaughton, the former sewing mistress in Aberfeldy who was bound for Ardeonaig. Catherine Ferguson had two daughters, one qualified to teach plain sewing and dressmaking, and the other was qualified to teach English reading, in 1827. [NRS.GD112.11.9.3.41]

FERGUSON, DAVID, son of Adam Ferguson of Woodhill, died in Fergus, Canada West, on 11 August 1855. [W.XVI.1688]

FERGUSON, DONALD, with his wife Mary, from Comrie, emigrated via Greenock aboard the Curlew bound for Quebec on 21 July 1818. [TNA.CO384/3.123-127]

FERGUSON, DUNCAN, with his wife Isabella and two children, from Balquhidder, emigrated via Greenock aboard the <u>Sophia of Ayr</u> bound for Quebec on 26 July 1818. [TNA.CO384/3.133-134]

FERGUSON, DUNCAN, with his wife Ann, from Comrie, emigrated via Greenock aboard the <u>Curlew</u> bound for Quebec on 21 July 1818. [TNA.CO384/3.123-127]

FERGUSON, FERGUS, of the Free Church in Kirkmichael, Blairgowrie, a petition, 1845. [NRS.GD112.51.189]

FERGUSON, JAMES, a thief in Perth Tolbooth, was banished for seven years on 13 September 1796. [PKA.B59.26.11.2]

FERGUSON, JAMES, born 1803 in Perthshire, died at Long Point, Quebec, on 1 January 1857. [EEC.210.21042]

FERGUSON, JAMES, with his wife Christine and two children, from Comrie, emigrated via Greenock aboard the <u>Curlew</u> bound for Quebec on 21 July 1818. [TNA.CO384/3.123-127]

FERGUSON, JAMES, of Middlehaugh, late of Jamaica, a testament, 1 June 1819, Comm. Dunkeld. [NRS]

FERGUSON, JAMES, born 1831, son of Peter Ferguson and his wife Margaret McKenzie, died in December 1863 in Australia. [Callander gravestone]

FERGUSON, JAMES SCOTT, son of Adam Ferguson of Woodhill, died in Woodhill, Canada West, on 7 July 1850. [AJ.5352][W.XI.1850]

FERGUSON, JANET, born 1855, daughter of William Ferguson and his wife Janet McKenzie, died in Pawtucket, Rhode Island, on 27 March 1889. [Coupar Angus gravestone]

FERGUSON, JOHN, alias James Robb, at Bridgend of Drumfork, guilty of forgery, was banished for seven years at Perth on 26 September 1795. [PKA.B59.26.11.5]

FERGUSON, JOHN, born 1762, emigrated from Perthshire in 1807, died at Hillsborough River, PEI?, in March 1842. [Halifax Journal, 28.3.1842]

FERGUSON, JOHN, born 1780, a labourer from Callendar, emigrated via Port Glasgow aboard the <u>Favourite of St John</u> bound for St John, New Brunswick, on 22 October 1815. [PANB.ms.RS23E.fo.9798]

FERGUSON, JOHN, born 1794, a smith from Kincairn, emigrated via Port Glasgow aboard the <u>Favourite of St John</u> bound for St John, New Brunswick, on 22 October 1815. [PANB.ms.RS23E.fo.9798]

FERGUSON, JOHN, a papermaker at East Mill of Auchterarder, accused of homicide in 1809. [NRS.JC26.1809.16]

FERGUSON, JOHN, born 1808, son of Robert Ferguson and his wife Janet Carmichael, died in Kyneton, Australia, on 10 August 1887. [Balquhidder gravestone]

FERGUSON, JOHN, a weaver and a dog-breaker at Longhall of Kilbryde, Dunblane, was accused of theft in 1812. [NRS.AD14.12.61]

FERGUSON, JOHN, with his wife Mary, from Comrie, emigrated via Greenock aboard the <u>Curlew</u> bound for Quebec on 21 July 1818. [TNA.CO384/3.123-127]

FERGUSON, JOHN, son of Peter Ferguson in Dunblane, was accused of administering drugs, in 1822. [NRS.AD14.22.105]

FERGUSON, JOHN, born 1794 in Perthshire, was naturalised in Cumberland County, North Carolina, in June 1821, [Cumberland County Court Records]

FERGUSON, JOHN, born 1830, a labourer in Perthshire, emigrated on the <u>John Bell</u> to Tasmania, landed in Hobart, Tasmania, on 4 December 1855. [SRA.TD292]

FERGUSON, MARGARET, born 1841, daughter of John Ferguson and his wife Catherine Stalker, died in Invercargill, New Zealand, on 13 March 1864. [Comrie gravestone]

FERGUSON, MARGARET MITCHELL, born 1847, wife of Thomas Fell, late of Coupar Angus, died in Kansas City, Kansas, on 7 November 1882. [S.12285]

FERGUSON, NEIL, a saddler and harness maker in Perth in 1812. [NRS.GD1.427.16/11]

FERGUSON, ROBERT, with his wife Christine, from Comrie, emigrated via Greenock aboard the <u>Curlew</u> bound for Quebec on 21 July 1818. [TNA.CO384/3.123-127]

FERGUSON, ROBERT OLIPHANT, born 1824 in Thornhill, Muthill, settled in New Braunfels, Texas, died there on 22 August 1850. [EEC.22034]

FERGUSON, WILLIAM, a plasterer in Callendar, was found guilty of assault and imprisoned for eight months in 1819. [NRS.JC11.60]

FERGUSON, WILLIAM, a manufacturer in Coupar Angus, and his wife Janet McKenzie, were parents of John Ferguson, born 1858, died in Pawtucket, Rhode Island, on 13 June 1890. [Coupar Angus Abbey gravestone]

FERGUSON, ....., son of George Ferguson of Pitfour, was born in Montreal, Quebec, on 29 July 1863. [W.XXIV.2636]

FERGUSON-BLAIR, A. J., born 1815, son of Adam Ferguson in Woodhill, Perthshire, a statesman who died in Canada on 1 January 1868. [GM.NS3/5.542]

FERNIE, JAMES, in Bankhead, Blairgowrie, accused of cattle stealing in 1817. [NRS.AD14.17.52]

FERNIE, PETER, born 1793 in Perthshire, an accountant who emigrated via Belfast to America, was naturalised in New York on 2 April 1821. [NARA]

FERRIER, THOMAS, from Perth, a theological student in 1810, emigrated to America. [UPC]

FINDLATOR, GEORGE, born 1821, son of James Findlator and his wife Janet McLauchlan, died in Sydney, Australia, on 30 April 1900. [Perth Greyfriars gravestone]

FINDLATOR, JOHN, in Blair Atholl, letters, 1823. [NRS.GD132.739]

FINDLATOR, ROBERT, son of James Findlator and his wife Janet McLauchlan, died in Bowen, Queensland, Australia, on 24 June 1891. [Perth Greyfriars gravestone]

FINDLAY, EDMUND JAMES FERGUSON, son of Alexander Ferguson in Moulin, a student at Marischal College, Aberdeen, in 1840s. [MCA]

FINLAY, JAMES, a brewer in Coupar Angus, dead by 1835. [NRS.S/H]

FINDLAY, JOHN, in Auchterarder, a sequestration petition, 1849. [NRS.CS279.290]

FISHER, DUNCAN, born 1753 in Dunkeld, emigrated to Canada, husband of Catherine Embury, died in 1820. [SC]

FISHER, Dr JAMES, born 1756, late surgeon in Montreal, Quebec, died in Dunkeld on 26 June 1822. [Dunkeld Cathedral gravestone]

FISHER, JAMES, from Breadalbane, a farmer at Long Point, Montreal, Quebec, died on 14 June 1832. [GA.4258]

FISHER, JAMES, born 1837, eldest son of Mr Fisher in St Colme's, Dunkeld, died in St Louis, Missouri, on 13 May 1872. [S.9002]

FISHER, JOHN, born in Killin, emigrated to Canada, settled in Hemingford, Quebec, in 1800. [SC]

FISHER, LOUISA, youngest daughter of Henry Fisher MD in Dunkeld, married Archibald Hamilton Campbell, a banker in Montreal, Quebec, on 3 April 1856. [GM.NS45.639]

FISHER, MALCOLM, with his wife Christine and five children, bound for Quebec on 21 July 1818. [TNA.CO384/3.123-127]

FISHER, MARGARET, born 1811, a housemaid, guilty of theft, was sentenced to transportation to the colonies, at Perth on 17 September 1833. [PKA.B59.26.11]

FISHER, Mrs MARY, from Balquhidder, emigrated via Greenock aboard the <u>Curlew</u> bound for Quebec on 21 July 1818. [TNA.CO384/3.123-127]

FLEMING, ROBERT, wood-keeper in Aberfeldy, a letter, 1805. [NRS.GD112.11.7.8.22]

FLETCHER, DUNCAN, in Killin, applied for the post of ground officer of the west end of Loch Tay in 1803. [NRS.GD112.11.7.6.10]

FOGO, GEORGE LAURIE, born 25 June 1847, son of John Laurie Fogo of Row, Perthshire, graduated MA from Glasgow University in 1867, minister of the Scots church in Dresden, Prussia, from 1871, returned to Scotland in 1883, died on 1 December 1912. [F.2.301]

FORBES, ALEXANDER, son of John Forbes in Monzie, Blair Atholl, accused of sheep stealing in 1837. [NRS.AD14.37.153]

FORBES, AMELIA, widow of David Beatson minister at Dunbarney, 1807. [NRS.E109/5]

FORBES, DAVID, born 1828 in Atholl, died in Transvaal on 14 November 1905. [Dowally gravestone]

FORBES, DONALD, born 1790, a labourer from Foss, emigrated aboard the Clarendon of Hull bound for Prince Edward Island in August 1808. [NSARM] [TNA.CO226.23]

FORBES, DUNCAN, [1827-1909], and his wife Grace McDonald, [1859-1932], parents of Annie Forbes, born 1878, died in Edmonton, Alberta, on 3 December 1917. [Aberfeldy gravestone]

FORBES, WILLIAM, in Callander, uncle of William Forbes in Vengeance, Prince Rupert Bay, Dominica in 1798. [NRS.RH1.2.808]

FORBES, WILLIAM, from Callander, a physician in Port Royal, Jamaica, letters, 1808-1809. [NRS.RH1/2.796]

FORBES, WILLIAM, a butcher in Doune, was accused of assault in 1809. [NRS.JC26.1809.17]; also, in 1816. [NRS.JC26.1816.26]

FORGAN, CATHERINE, widow of Charles Patullo, farmer in Broadley, Errol, now New Scone, a Declarator of Marriage, 1820. [NRS.CC8.6.2027]

FORESTER, SOMERVILLE, in Westmoreland, Cornwall, Jamaica, died 1 October 1804, brother of David Forester of Polder in Perthshire, testament, 1811, Comm. Edinburgh. [NRS]

FRASER, ALEXANDER, in Inver, Little Dunkeld, a victim of forgery in 1831. [NRS.AD14.31.65]

FRASER, CHARLES, born 1800 in Blair Atholl, died in Canada on 22 July 1894, his wife, Christine Douglas, born 1804 in Blair Atholl, died in Canada on 24 December 1876. [White Lake Community cemetery, Renfrew County, Ontario, gravestone]

FRASER, DANIEL, minister of the Free Church in Scone, a letter, 1845. [NRS.GD112.51.186]

FRASER, DONALD, a heckler in Crieff, dead by 1797, father of John Fraser in America. [NRS.S/H]

FRASER, FANNY MARIA, youngest daughter of Alexander Garden Fraser in New York, married Reverend John Pirie from Edinburgh, in Kenmore on 12 June 1861. [AJ.5919]

FRASER, JAMES, in Perth Tolbooth accused of theft, house-breaking and reset, was sentenced to be hanged in 1819. [NRS.JC26.1819.85]

FRASER, JAMES, born 1745 in Perthshire, died in Halifax, Nova Scotia, on 2 December 1822. [Free Press.10.12.1822]

FRASER, JAMES, millwright in Dowally, a letter re the sawmill in Killin, 1830. [NRS.GD112.74.105]

FRASER, JAMES FYFE, born 1827 in Coupar Angus, son of John Fraser and his wife Cecilia Fyfe, a merchant in New York, died in Perth on 20 August 1856. [ANY]

FRASER, JOHN, a painter in Perth, dead by 1841, uncle of William Johnston Fraser in New York. [NRS.S/H]

FRASER, JOHN, a wright in Dunning, dead by 1852, father of William Fraser a minister in Hampden, New York. [NRS.S/H]

FRASER, JOHN, born 1846, son of John Fraser and his wife Ann Ferguson, died in Ontario on 2 October 1869. [Moulin, gravestone]

FRASER, PATRICK, brother of John Fraser in Perth, settled on Long Island in the Bahamas, probate March 1795, PCC. [TNA]

FREER, GEORGE, of Freeland, a tack of part of the burgh muir of Perth in 1802. [PKA.B59.25.3.8]

FULLAR, JAMES, a distiller in Perth, testament, 1794, Comm. St Andrews. [NRS]

FULLARTON, C., daughter of Alexander Fullarton, a land surveyor in Perth, married Robert Bowden, from South Carolina, in Glasgow on 1 February 1802. [SM.64.181]

FULLARTON, JOHN, born 1787, a labourer from Buttergask, Cargill, emigrated via Greenock aboard the William of New York bound for New York on 4 September 1817, landed there on 17 October 1817. [NY Municipal Archives] [NY Commercial Advertiser, 18.10.1817]

GALL, FREDERICK, in Barlach Loan, Coupar Angus, a victim of mobbing and rioting there in 1829. [NRS.JC26.1829.23]

GALLITLY, JAMES, born 1792, a labourer from Pittensorn, Little Dunkeld, emigrated via Greenock aboard the William of New York bound for New York on 4 September 1817, landed there on 17 October 1817. [NY Municipal Archives] [NY Commercial Advertiser, 18.10.1817]

GALLATLY, JOHN, High Street, Perth, a victim of theft in 1832. [NRS.AD14.29.129]

GALLOWAY, EUPHAN, widow of John Howie, in Perth, testament, 1800, Comm. St Andrews. [NRS]

GALLOWAY, JAMES, a land surveyor in Blairgowrie, 1791-1807. [NRS.S96.2476]

GALLOWAY, JOHN, in East Carse of Trowan, was accused of fire raising in 1808. [NRS.JC26.1808.49]; and was outlawed. [NRS.JC11.49]

GALLOWAY, THOMAS, in Dovecotland, Perth, was accused of theft in 1801. [NRS.JC11.45]

GARDINER, JAMES, born 1832, son of Captain John Gardiner of Carse Grange, a merchant in Abingdon, USA, died on 15 September 1868. [Errol gravestone]

GARDINER, JOHN, a baker in Perth, dead by 1798, brother of Andrew Gardiner in Douanville, Jamaica. [NRS.S/H]

GARDINER, Mrs, wife of John Gardiner formerly a tenant farmer in Pitcaithly, Perthshire, died in Charleston, South Carolina, in December 1806. [SM.69.638]

GARDNER, ANDREW, in Duanscale, Trelawney, Jamaica, brother of John Gardner a baker in Perth, a disposition, 1797. [NRS.RD3.278.840]

GARDNER, DAVID, a maltman in Perth, testament, 1791, Comm. St Andrews. [NRS]

GARDNER, JOHN, a baker and bailie of Perth, testament, 1797, Comm. St Andrews. [NRS]

GARDNER, WILLIAM, a tailor in Perth, testament, 1793, Comm. St Andrews. [NRS]

GARDNER, WILLIAM, the younger, a tailor in Perth, testament, 1793, Comm. St Andrews. [NRS]

GARVIE, WILLIAM, minister at Aberdalgie in 1830. [NRS.CS313.418]

GARVIE, WILLIAM, a manufacturer in Bankfoot, died in July 1841, father of Joseph Garvie at Owen Sound, Ontario. [NRS.S/H.1869]

GEDDES, JOHN, son of Alexander Geddes, [1777-1859]. And his wife Elizabeth Gregory. [1784-1838], died in America aged 20. [Perth, Greyfriars, gravestone]

GEEKIE, WILLIAM, a bleacher and bone crusher in Balgersher, Coupar Angus, 1840. [NRS.CS280.26.20]62.18]

GELLATLY, JAMES, in Haughmill of Rattray, a victim of theft in 1835. [NRS.AD14.35.110]

GENTLE, ALEXANDER, third son of Alexander Gentle in Dunkeld, died in Demerara on 17 December 1818. [S.62.18]

GENTLE, ANDREW, a farmer in Logie, Perthshire, a victim of robbery in 1832. [NRS.AD14.32.342]

GENTLE, ANDREW, a brewer in Dunblane, versus his wife Isobel Key, daughter of Robert Key a tenant in Touch, a divorce in 1792. [NRS.CC8.6.877]; emigrated to America, settled in Hemingford, Quebec, in 1801. [SC]

GENTLE, WILLIAM, a planter in Claredon, Jamaica, before 1807. [PKA.B59.38.6.247]

GEORGE, JAMES, from Auchterarder, emigrated to America in 1820s, minister in Scarborough, Ontario, later Principal of Queen's College, Kingston, Ontario. [UPC]

GEORGE, Reverend JAMES, born 8 November 1800, son of James George a farmer in Muckhart, was educated at Glasgow University in 1823, a minister in Philadelphia, Fort Covington, New York and in Ontario, died there on 26 August 1870. [MAGU.337][UPC]

GIBB, CHARLES LYALL, born 12 September 1857, son of David Gibb and his wife Helen Valentine, died in Seattle, Washington, on 15 November 1904. [Abernethy gravestone]

GIBSON, ALEXANDER, son of James Gibson and his wife Jean Cumming, in Lethendy, testament, 1792, Comm. St Andrews. [NRS]

GIBSON, ELIZABETH, from Perth, guilty of infanticide, was sentenced to transportation to the colonies for fourteen years in 1803. [PKA.B59.26.11.2]

GIBSON, WILLIAM, son of Alexander Gibson master of Perth Academy, a servant of John Ritchie in Virgin Valley, St James, Jamaica, from 1797 to 1800. [PKA.B59.37.4.29]; an overseer om Somerton Estate, Jamaica, died on 1 December 1805. [SM.68.238]

GIBSON, WILLIAM, in Croft of Kincladdie, a bond of caution for Peter Chalmer a wright in Dunning in 1803. [NRS.CS271.767]

GILCHRIST, JOHN, born 1819, was found guilty of forgery in Perth in 1814 and sentenced to transportation to the colonies for 14 years. [NRS.GD1.959]

GILLAN, JAMES, born 1820 in Perth, died in August 1842 aboard the brig Diamond bound from Berbice for New Brunswick. [St Andrews Standard, 26.8.1842]

GILLESPIE, JAMES, a merchant in Perth, testament, 1799, Comm. St Andrews. [NRS]

GILLESPIE, JAMES, in Dunblane, a letter, 1800. [NRS.GD1.1398.11.9]

GILLESPIE, JOHN, in Dunblane, was accused of discharging a firearm and theft in 1824. [NRS.AD14.24.364]

GILMOUR, ROBERT, a weaver from Blackford, now in Camden Town, London, versus Helen Anderson from Blackford, a decree of divorce, 1839. [NRS.CS46.1839.193]

GLASS, ANN, daughter of George Glass in Abernethy, a victim of crime in 1823. [NRS.JC26.1823.198]

GLASS, HELEN, widow of Dr John Stewart in Blair Atholl, dead by 1853, mother of James Alexander Stewart in New York. [NRS.S/H]

GLASS, ROBERT, a prisoner in Perth Tolbooth, petitioned for banishment in August 1799. [PKA.B59.26.11.2]

GLEN, CATHERINE, born 1818, guilty of theft, was sentenced to transportation to the colonies for seven years, in 1832 in Perth. [PKA.B59.26.11.3.6]

GLOAG, JOHN, of Greenhill, born 1738, died in Perth on 2 June 1820. [SM.6.190]

GLOAG, MATTHEW, [1797-1860], a merchant in Perth, and his wife Margaret Brown, [1797-1847], parents of Joseph Gloag who died in Dobbo, New South Wales, Australia, on 29 July 1892. [Greyfriars gravestone, Perth]

GOLD, DAVID, a coachmaker in Demerara, later in Crieff, testament, 29 October 1829. [NRS.CC7.9.4.412]

GORDON, DONALD, born 1763, a farmer from Perthshire, with his wife Christian born 1772, daughter Isabella born 1797, son Henry born 1798, son James born 1800, and son James born 1802, emigrated via Port Glasgow aboard the Commerce bound for Pictou, Nova Scotia, on 10 August 1803. [NLS.ms1053.104-109]

GORDON, JAMES, in Dunkeld, a victim of assault in 1821. [NRS.AD14.21.89]

GORDON, JEAN, wife of Thomas Ross a soldier of the Breadalbane Fencibles, guilty of mobbing, was banished for three years, in Perth in 1796. [PKA.B59.26.11.2]

GORDON, or GARDINER, JOHN, a shop-breaker, was sentenced to fourteen years transportation to the colonies, at Perth on 22 September 1798. [SM]

GORDON, ROBERT, in Milnathort, Kinross, a victim of rioting in Dollar in 1837. [NRS.AD14.37.475]

GORE, JOHN, born 1770, a labourer from Strathbraan, emigrated aboard the Clarendon of Hull bound for Prince Edward Island in August 1808. [NSARM] [TNA.CO226.23]

GORRIE, ARCHIBALD, in Annat Cottage, Errol, session clerk of Kinfauns Free Church, a letter, 1845. [NRS.GD112.51.186]

GORRIE, DAVID, born in Perth, died in Camden, South Carolina, on 23 March 1821. [Camden Gazette: 29.3.1821]

GORRIE, DUNCAN, born 1773, died in Glengarry, North America, by 1847. [Monzie gravestone]

GORRIE, ELIZABETH, daughter of James Gorrie, [1800-1860], and his wife Janet Patton, [1811-1878], wife of ……. Bennet, settled in Timaru, New Zealand. [Methven gravestone]

GORRIE, GEORGE, born 1840, son of George Gorrie and his wife Jean Cathro, died in Queensland, Australia, on 25 July 1880. [Rattray gravestone]

GORRIE, HELEN, born 1799, died in Glengarry, North America, on 7 March 1868. [Monzie gravestone]

GORRIE, JOHN, born 1780, a merchant from Moneydie, emigrated via Greenock aboard the William of New York bound for New York on 4 September 1817, landed there on 17 October 1817. [NY Municipal Archives] [NY Commercial Advertiser, 18.10.1817]

GORRIE, JOSEPH, from Perthshire, settled in Wilmington, North Carolina, died in 1830. [Williams pp, UNC]

GOULD, JAMES, born 1799 in Crieff, son of John Gould and his wife Mary Bruce, a stonecutter in Little Falls, Herkimer County, New York, married Anna Eva Garter on 9 February 1837, probate 31 October 1845. [Herkimer County Wills, Volume H, fo.115]

GOURLAY, JOHN, farmer of Over Kinfauns, testament, 1799, Comm. St Andrews. [NRS]

GOW, JOHN, a tenant at the bridge end of Strowan, versus Margaret Forbes in Tullimet, Logerait, a process of divorce in 1811. [NRS.CC8.6.1442]

GOW, JOHN, with his wife Jane, from Comrie, emigrated via Greenock aboard the Curlew bound for Quebec on 21 July 1818. [TNA.CO384/3.123-127]

GOW, JOHN, born 1850 in Perthshire, died in Buffalo, New York, on 26 April 1862. [S.8990]

GOW, NEIL, born 1727, 'the famous fiddler', died at Inver near Dunkeld in 1807. [AJ.1.3.1807]

GOW, THOMAS, and his wife Jane Robie, parents of William Gow, born 1854, died in Johannesburg, South Africa, on 16 August 1898. [Little Dunkeld gravestone]

GOWANS, JOHN, in Tennessee, heir to his mother Jean Clerk, wife of Peter Gowans in Crieff, in 1829. [NRS.S/H]

GRAHAM, JAMES, fourth son of Robert Burdon Graham of Feddel, was educated at Glasgow University in 1788, died in Jamaica on 16 January 1806. [Caribbeana.4.17]

GRAHAM, JOHN, second son of John Graham of Drunkie, died in Trelawney, Jamaica, on 30 November 1802. [EA.4090.03]

GRAHAM, JOHN, in Ardoch, a letter, 1802. [NRS.GD1.393.12]

GRAHAM, JOHN, from Monzie, emigrated via Greenock aboard the Portaferry bound for Quebec in May 1832. [Quebec Mercury, 13.6.1832]

GRAHAM, THOMAS WILLIAM, youngest son of John Graham of Drunkie, died in Jamaica, in August 1803. [DPCA.70]

GRANT, DONALD, son of John Grant in Easter Balnauld of Broughdairg, Kilmichael, was accused of fire-raising in 1801. [NRS.JC26.1801.48]

GRANT, FRANCIS, in Jamaica, heir to his brother John Grant of Kilgraston, the Chief Justice of Jamaica, in 1794. [NRS.S/H]

GRANT, GEORGE, an Excise officer in Auchterarder, versus John Flockhart, a writer in Perth, 1822. [NRS.CS.271.34]

GRANT, JAMES, former Quartermaster of the Perthshire Light Dragoons, died in Kempshot Pen, Jamaica, in 1802. [EA.4041.02]

GRANT, JOHN, of Kilgraston, Chief Justice of Jamaica, dead by 1794. [NRS.S/H]

GRANT, JOHN, of Kilgraston, married Margaret Gray, second daughter of Lord Gray, at Kilfauns Castle on 20 June 1820. [SM.86.94]

GRANT, PATRICK, a weaver in Perth, an indenture, 1791. [PKA.B59.29.94]

GRAY, ANDREW, a victim of assault in Killin in 1831. [NRS.AD14.31.47]

GRAY, DAVID, a victim of assault in Killin in 1831. [NRS.AD14.31.47]

GRAY, PATRICK, born 1746, settled on Friendship Estate, Hanover, Jamaica, died at Glen Doick House, Perthshire, on 24 July 1806. [Kinfauns gravestone]

GRAY, WILLIAM, a merchant and Provost of Perth, testament, 1790, Comm. St Andrews. [NRS]

GRAY, WILLIAM, born 10 November 1818 in Inchture, son of William Gray, [1762-1827], and his wife Elspeth Wynd, [1779-1854], a weaver and a mason, married Margaret McBryde on 4 October 1844, emigrated to America in 1850, a builder in Philadelphia, Pennsylvania, died there on 31 July 1891. [Longforgan gravestone] [AP]

GREENHILL, PETER, son of James Greenhill and his wife Ann Duncan, died in St Louis on 25 April 1875. [Abernethy gravestone]

GREIG, JAMES, son of Alexander Greig a schoolmaster in Perth, a student at Marischal College, Aberdeen, in 1838. [MCA]

GREGOR, or MCGREGOR, CHARLES, son of John Gregor, a mason at Bridge of Earn, Dunbarney, was accused of assault in 1821. [NRS.AD14.21.78]

GREGOR, MARY, in Braehead of Millhole, Meffan, testament, 1800, Comm. St Andrews. [NRS]

GREIG, DAVID, of Little Tillerie, Orwell, Kinross, testament, 1796, Comm. St Andrews. [NRS]

GREIG, EUPHEMIA, born 1826, daughter of Charles Greig and his wife Grace Saunders, died in Euchea, Victoria, Australia, on 3 July 1872. [Collace gravestone][Coupar Angus gravestone]

GREIG, Miss MARGARET, keeper of a boarding school and a day school in Perth, a petition, 1819. [PKA.B59.24.6.140]

GUNN, THOMAS, a minister in Madderty, Crieff, a letter, 1845. [NRS.GD112.51.186]

GUNN, WILLIAM, born 1818, a merchant in Canada West, died in Perth on 7 December 1844. [Perth, Greyfriars, gravestone]

GUTHRIE, ALEXANDER, in Doune, was accused of assault in 1816. [NRS.JC26.1816.26]

HALKETT, PETER, a tenant in Pitcur, sederunt book, 1842. [NRS.CS96.4395]

HALLY, ANDREW, a glazier in Crieff, accounts, 1806-1810. [NRS.GD241.682]

HALLY, DAVID, a glazier in Crieff, accounts, 1806-1810. [NRS.GD241.682]

HAY, ALEXANDER BALCARRES, in Jamaica, son and heir of Agnes Ogilvy, wife of John Hay of Pitfour, in 1807. [NRS.S/H]

HAY, ALEXANDER, a saddler and harness maker in Perth in 1812. [NRS.GD1.427.16/11]

HAY, CHARLES, of Beechhill, heir of Gilbert Hay of Ballindoch in 1814. [PKA.B59.38.6.262]

HAY, JOHN, a tailor in Dunning, was accused of forgery in 1814. [NRS.JC26.1814.3]

HAY, Reverend JOHN, died in Kincardine, Canada West, on 13 July 1866. [Perth, Greyfriars, gravestone]

HEDDERICK, WILLIAM, a drover and cattle dealer in Blackford, 1802. [NRS.CS233.SEQN.H.1.11]

HEDDERWICK, MARJORY, in Perthshire, found guilty of infanticide was sentenced to transportation to the colonies for seven years in 1803. [PKA.B59.26.11.2]

HEMPSEED, ANDREW, born on Caldhame Farm, Blairlogie, a farm labourer in Kinross, was accused of sheep stealing from Jerah farm, Logie, Perthshire, in 1832. [NRS.AD14.32.342]

HENDERSON, ANN, daughter of Thomas Henderson in Abernethy, a victim of crime in 1823. [NRS.JC26.1823.198]

HENDERSON, ARABELLA HAMILTON, youngest daughter of Colonel Henderson of Foswell Bank, married Richard Haifne of the Royal Staff Corps, in Port Henderson, Jamaica, on 17 December 1828. [S.936.834]

HENDERSON, HENRY, accused of housebreaking and assault in High Street, Blairgowrie, 1831. [NRS.JC26.1831.211]

HENDERSON, HENRY, of Kingston, Canada West, formerly in Perth, married Margaret Bruce Davidson, daughter of David Davidson in Coupar Angus, in Montreal, Quebec, on 30 March 1864. [DPCA.4214]

HENDERSON, JEAN, married Donald McDonald, a servant of the Earl of Kelly on 14 October 1794 in Kinclaven, a process of divorce in 1800. [NRS.CC8.6.1076]

HENDERSON, JOHN, born 1817 in Dunblane, a labourer, was accused of theft in 1838. [NRS.AD14.38.97]

HENDERSON, Reverend MATTHEW, born in Kinross, a minister in Charties and Buffalo, Pittsburgh, Pennsylvania, died in October 1795. [GM.65.1112]

HENDERSON, STEPHEN, settled in New Orleans, Louisianan, by 1831. [Dunblane gravestone]

HENDRY, DAVID, born 1838, son of John Hendry and his wife Jane Baird, died in Adelaide, South Australia, on 1 April 1876. [Abernethy gravestone]

HENRY, ANDREW, born 1777 in Auchterarder, died in Charleston, South Carolina, on 25 September 1807. [Old Scots gravestone, Charleston]

HEPBURN, DAVID, in Scone, a victim of theft in 1837. [NRS.AD14.37.163]

HEPBURN, JOHN, a weaver in Perth, dead by 1846. [NRS.S/H]

HEPBURN, ROBERT, born 1784, son of Henry Hepburn, [1762-1832], a builder in Perth, and his wife Jean Forrester, [1760-1843], died in Tobago on 7 September 1801. [Greyfriars gravestone, Perth]

HEPBURN, ROBERT, a shipmaster in Errol, later a mariner in Dundee, testament, 1804. [NRS.CC3.13.137]

HERON, JOHN, a partner of the Flax Spinning Mill at Milton of Rattray, versus David Peter, messenger at arms in Blairgowrie, 1823. [NRS.CS271.48]

HILL, JAMES, born 1821, son of Job Hill, a private in the 13th Regiment of Foot, and his wife Catherine, was accused of theft in 1835. [NRS.AD14.35.179]

HILL, JOHN, son of James Hill mason at Deans Cross, Caputh, a clerk and messenger at arms in Dunkeld, was accused of forgery in 1827. [NRS.AC14.27.198]

HILL, THOMAS, in Milnathort, Kinross, a victim of housebreaking in 1837. [NRS.AD14.37.2053]

HONEY, JOHN ADAMSON, at Inchture Manse, letters, 1842-1845. [NRS.GD508.9.4]

HORNE, ELIZABETH ANN, daughter of Thomas Horne and his wife Ann Anderson, died in Dunedin, New Zealand, on 23 November 1860. [Invergowrie gravestone]

HORNE, JESSIE, born 1837, daughter of Colin Horne, [1808-1847], a gardener in Balruddery, and his wife Margaret McHardy, [1813-1900], died in New York, in February 1864. [Longforgan gravestone]

HORNE, THOMAS, born 1840, son of Colin Horne, [1808-1847], a gardener in Balruddery, and his wife Margaret McHardy, [1813-1900], died in Jersey City, USA, in February 1879. [Longforgan gravestone]

HOUSTON, ALEXANDER, a dyker in Craigow, was accused on the murder of George Beath near Kinross on 28 July 1802. [NRS.JC26.1803.14]

HOWDEN, MARION, second daughter of John Howden in Nether Braco, married William Balgonie, in Windsor Villa, Georgetown, Demerara, on 15 November 1870. [S.8545]

HOWIE, MARY, wife of David Scott tenant in Ardler, petitioned for loco parentis in 1813, he being in Aberdeen Lunatic Asylum. [NRS.CS97.107.21]

HUIE, Reverend JOHN, from Perth, died in Geelong, Victoria, Australia, on 15 February 1864. [AJ.6068]

HUNTER, CHARLES, in Argaith, Errol, was the victim of theft in 1831. [NRS.AD41.31.55]

HUNTER, THOMAS, third son of Charles Hunter in Glencarse, died in Fergus, Upper Canada, on 8 January 1853. [EEC.22392] [S.12.2.1853]

HUTCHISON, JOHN, born 1769, a blacksmith in Blairgowrie, was accused of housebreaking and theft in 1819. [NRS.AD14.19.304; JC26.1819.85]

HUTCHISON, MARY, spouse of John Easson in Balfour, a prisoner in Perth Tolbooth, was accused of arson at Lint Mill of the Kirkton of Abernyte in 1801. [NRS.JC26.1801.48/5]

HUTCHISON, WILLIAM ORROCK, son of John Hutchison and his wife Catherine....., died in Toronto, Canada, on 25 May 1852. [Perth, Wellshill, gravestone]

HUTTON, ANDREW, born 1815, a machine-maker in Perth, was accused of the rape of Mary McPherson, daughter of Jean McGregor or McPherson, a widow in Pitcairngreen, Redgorton, in 1835. [NRS.AD14.35.86]

HUTTON, ANN, in Perth, dead by 1851. [NRS.S/H]

IMRIE, DAVID, in Errol, a victim of forgery in 1832. [NRS.AD14.32.18]

IMRIE, JAMES, a shoemaker in Aberfeldy, was accused of forgery in 1831. [NRS.AD14.31.65]

IRVINE, ROBERT, second son of Reverend Dr Irvine in Little Dunkeld, died in Garth, Trinidad, in March 1830. [BM.28.571]

IRVING, GEORGE, a merchant in Blairgowrie, testament, 1799, Comm. St Andrews. [NRS]

ISDALE, JANET, wife of John Craigie a baker at Bridge of Earn, Dumbarney, testament, 1796, Comm. St Andrews. [NRS]

ISLES, GEORGE, in Cargill, a victim of theft in 1837. [NRS.AD14.37.100]

ISLES, JAMES, born 1752 in Perthshire, died in Halifax, Nova Scotia, on 2 May 1827. [Acadian Recorder, 5.5.1827]

ISLES, JAMES, born 1837, son of William Isles, [1802-1873], and his wife Isabella Howie, [1806-1888], died on 3 November 1888 in Insulae Clayfield, Brisbane, Queensland, Australia. [New Scone gravestone]

JACK, ALEXANDER, a merchant in Perth, died 24 July 1810, uncle of George Young in Fitzroy, Canada West. [NRS.S/H.1863]

JACK, ANDREW, in Dunning, a victim of assault in 1829. [NRS.AD14.29.141]

JACK, ELIZABETH, wife of William Hutton a sawyer in Dunning, accused of theft 1818. [NRS.AD14.18.31]

JACKSON, BARBARA, from Perthshire, was sentenced to transportation to the colonies for seven years in 1804. [PKA.B59.26.11.2]

JACKSON, JOSEPH, son of Thomas Jackson, [1756-1827], and his wife Margaret Grimman, [1762-1838], settled in Montreal, Quebec. [Kilspindie gravestone]

JACKSON, WILLIAM, [1849-1878], a plasterer, and his wife Agnes Ireland, [1849-1875], parents of George Jackson, born 1870, died in November 1873, buried in Phillipsburg, New Jersey. [Coupar Angus gravestone]

JAMIESON, ELIZABETH, in Perth Tolbooth accused of theft and reset, sentenced to twelve months in prison, 1819. [NRS.JC26.1819.85]

JAMIESON, JOHN, born 1768, minister of the Scone Burgher Church from 1791 until his death in 1853, was awarded a Doctor of Divinity degree from Jefferson College, USA, in 1841. [NRS.CH3.1184.16]

JAMIESON, STEWART, in Perth Tolbooth accused of theft and reset, sentenced to twelve months in prison, 1819. [NRS.JC26.1819.85]

JOHNSTONE, or JAMIESON, ELIZABETH, in Barrack Street, Perth, was accused of theft in 1837. [NRS.AD14.37.100]

JOHNSTONE, PATRICK, a butcher and merchant in Perth, testament, 1799, Comm. St Andrews. [NRS]

JOHNSTONE, ROBERT CRAWFORD, born 1795, a wright in Kirkton of Foss, was accused of uttering false notes in 1825. [NRS.AD14.25.142]

JOLLY, DAVID LEITCH, born 1833, son of David L. Jolly a banker in Perth, married Margaret Elizabeth Stuart MacGregor, youngest daughter of Robert MacGregor in Campbeltown, in the British Consulate in Mexico on 2 April 1860. [DC.23504] [W.21.2196] [S.1538]; a daughter was born in Tampico on 2 November 1873, [S.9449]; he was accidentally killed in Tampico, Mexico on 10 December 1882. [S.12300]

JOLLY, ROBERT KEITH, fourth son of William Gairdner Jolly, died in Tampico, Mexico, on 30 May 1867. [S.7484]

JOYCE, alias FORREST, ALEXANDER, a pickpocket and thief, was sentenced to transportation to the colonies for fourteen years, in Perth on 1 October 1812. [SM.84.798].

JUST, JOHN, born in Perthshire, settled in New York by 1868, died there on 14 September 1893. [ANY]

JUSTICE, DAVID, in New Scone, a victim of theft in 1829. [NRS.AD14.29.129]

KAY, ROBERT, a carrier in Alyth, imprisoned in Perth Tolbooth accused of theft at the house of Joseph Dryburgh at the Boat of Badmoney in 1801. [NRS.JC26.1801.48/4]

KEAN, EDWARD, was found guilty of passing false coin in Blairgowrie and sentenced to 18 months hard labour in 1837. [NRS.JC26.1837.467]

KEAY, DAVID, born 1816, son of William Keay and his wife Ann Soutar, died in Mexico in August 1865. [Lethendy gravestone]

KEAY, GRANT, born 1805, widow of Samuel Hood in Luncarty, died in Buffalo, New York, on 15 December 1890. [Perthshire Weekly News, 1860]

KEAY, MARGARET, servant to Peter Duncan at Walton of Balbrogie, Coupar Angus, accused of child murder in 1816. [NRS JC26.1816.139]

KEAY, MCKENZIE, and MARTIN, merchants in Perth, trading with the Baltic lands from 1845 to 1856. [PKA.B59.37.6.1]

KEIR, JOHN, in Kinnaird, testament, 1799, Comm. St Andrews. [NRS]

KEIR, or ANDERSON, MARGARET, in Kinross, accused of inciting a child to steal in 1812. [NRS.AD14.12.113]

KEIR, MARGARET, in Ball's land, High Street, Perth, accused of exposing a child to the danger of its life in 1820, sentenced to four months in Perth Tolbooth in 1820. [NRS.AC14.20.141; JC26.1820.115]

KEIR, PETER, a meal seller in Perth, testament, 1793, Comm. St Andrews. [NRS]

KELT, JAMES, from the Carse of Gowrie, a member of the Scots Charitable Society of Boston, New England, in 1817. [SCS/NEHGS]

KELTIE, JOHN, in the Crook of Devon, grandfather of John Keltie a wright in America in 1816. [NRS.CS17.1.36/132]

KEMP, DAVID MALCOLM, born 1810, son of James Kemp, a land surveyor, who died at the Bay of Islands, New Zealand, on 15 March 1841. [Trinity Gask gravestone]

KEMP, WILLIAM, a victualler and feuar in Crieff, dead by 1847, uncle of John Kemp a merchant in New Orleans, Louisiana. [NRS.S/H]

KENNEDY, or ROBERTSON, CATHERINE, in Rattray, accused of sheep stealing in 1839. [NRS.AD14.39.120]

KENNEDY, CHARLES NEIL, a surgeon from Pitlochry, died on St Vincent on 4 January 1824. [FH.111]

KENNEDY, DONALD, born 1758, a farmer from Perthshire, with his wife Margaret born 1768, daughter Janet born 1793, son John born 1795, son Robert born 1797, and son Donald born 1800, emigrated via Port Glasgow aboard the Commerce bound for Pictou, Nova Scotia, on 10 August 1803. [NLS.ms1053.104-109]

KENNEDY, DUNCAN, born 1773, a labourer from Foss, with his wife Margaret born 1786, and daughter Jane born 1807, emigrated aboard the Clarendon of Hull bound for Prince Edward Island in August 1808. [NSARM] [TNA.CO226.23]

KENNEDY, JAMES, a grocer in Perth, testament, 1796, Comm. St Andrews. [NRS]

KENNEDY, JAMES, guilty of forgery in Perth was sentenced to transportation to the colonies for fourteen years in 1815. [NRS.GD1.959]

KENNEDY, JOHN, born 1770, a labourer from Foss, with his wife Janett born 1778, daughter Janet born 1800, son Donald born 1802, daughter Elizabeth born 1804, and son Duncan born 1807, emigrated aboard the Clarendon bound for Prince Edward Island in August 1808. [NSARM]

KENNEDY, JOHN, with his wife Margaret and two children, from Dull, emigrated via Greenock aboard the Curlew bound for Quebec on 21 July 1818. [TNA.CO384/3.123-127]

KENNEDY, JOHN, born 1818, in Aberargie, Abernethy, was accused of poaching in 1836. [NRS.AD14.36.457]

KENNEDY, JOSEPH, born 1794, a labourer from Foss, emigrated aboard the Clarendon of Hull bound for Prince Edward Island in August 1808. [NSARM] [TNA.CO226.23]

KENNEDY, Reverend THOMAS, in St Madoes, a letter, 1803. [PKA.B59.28.199]

KERR, ELIZABETH, a thief in Callander, 1832. [NRS.AD14.32.9]

KETTLE, ANDREW, tenant in Easter Moncrief, testaments, 1793, Comm. St Andrews. [NRS]

KETTLE, ANDREW, a maltman in Perth, testament, 1796, Comm. St Andrews. [NRS]

KIDD, DAVID, in Blairgowrie, a victim of forgery in 1824. [NRS.AD14.24.101]

KIDD, JAMES, died in Jamaica, leaving a legacy for the poor of Scone in 1820. [PKA.B59.38.56]

KIDD, ROBERT, born 1826, died in Australia on 16 February 1853. [Longforgan gravestone]

KILLEAR, PETER, a weaver in Perth, testament, 1792, Comm. St Andrews. [NRS]

KING, CHARLES, born 1795, a thief who was sentenced at Perth to transportation to the colonies for fourteen years in October 1832. [PKA.B59.26.11.3.6]

KING, JOHN, born 1833, son of James King and his wife Isabella Sharp, died in Rio de Janeiro, Brazil, on 22 June 1850. [Greyfriars gravestone, Perth]

KING, PETER, and Christy Ann McColl, both from Perthshire, were married in St John, New Brunswick, on 22 March,1807. [New Brunswick Courier, 27.3.1830]

KINLOCH, CHARLES YOUNG, last of Gourdie, born 8 September 1863, died in Vernon, Canada, on 26 March 1930. [Clunie gravestone]

KINLOCH, DAVID, of Gourdie, the Collector of Cess and Rogue Money for Perthshire in 1807. [PKA.B59.24.11. 190]

KINMONTH, DAVID, in Dunning, 1843. [NRS.CS271.67]

KINMONTH, JAMES, in Dunblane, a petition, 1823. [NRS.CS27.71.3]

KINROSS, JOHN, a vintner in Dunblane, died 31 May 1827. [NRS.S/H]

KIRK, EBENEZER, born 1832 in Kinross, died in Montgomery, Alabama, on 1 August 1866. [DA.1673]

KIRK, Reverend JOHN, tacksman of Kaimknow farm, Glen Devon, a victim of assault in 1822. [NRS.AD14.22.58]

KISSEN, ANDREW, in Lethendy, Blairgowrie, a letter, 1845. [NRS.GD112.51.186]

KYNOCH, JANET, born 1806, in Dowally, a thief. 1848. [NRS.AD14.48.265]

LAING, DAVID, born 1849, son of Robert Laing and his wife Margaret Miller, died in Hartford, Connecticut, on 18 December 1870. [Alyth gravestone]

LAING, ROBERT, from Abernethy, a minister in Duns, later a pastor in Buffalo, Washington County, Pennsylvania, in 1791, in South Argyle in 1805, in Bovina, Delaware County, New York, in 1814, died on 29 May 1839. [UPC.1.339]

LAMB, ALEXANDER, [1838-1907], and his wife Isabella Butter, [1836-1914], parents of Andrew Lamb, born 1875, died in Montreal, Quebec, on 28 September 1916. [Dunkeld Cathedral gravestone]

LAMB, ANN, daughter of George Lamb of Kercock, Kinclaven, was accused of child murder in 1800, case dismissed. [NRS.JC26.1800.60]

LAMMIE, JOHN, master of the <u>Amelia of Perth,</u> testament, 19 November 1836, Comm. Edinburgh. [NRS]

LAMOND, DONALD, son of Patrick Lamond in Whitemyre, was apprenticed to George Buist a saddler and harness maker in Perth for five years, 1805. [NRS.GD1.427.16/8]

LAMONT, NEIL, an innkeeper in Balnald, Strathtummel, was accused of the culpable homicide of James Stewart in 1837. [NRS.AD14.37.162]

LANGLANDS, ANNA & JEAN, in Perth, testament, 1800, Comm. St Andrews. [NRS]

LAUDER, JOHN ALEXANDER, born 1849, died in Elphinstone, Manitoba, on 27 September 1897. [Monzievaird gravestone]

LAWRENCE, WILLIAM, born 1822 in Blackford, settled in Merrimac, Iowa, died in Auchterarder on 9 December 1889. [Blackford gravestone]

LAWSON, AGNES, widow of John McGregor a labourer in Rattray, was accused of concealment of pregnancy and child murder in 1816. [NRS.JC26.1816.16]

LAWSON, GEORGE, born 1859, son of Robert Lawson, [1818-1899], a joiner, and his wife Jane McKenzie, [1822-1888], died in Cleveland, Ohio, on 7 May 1898. [Coupar Angus gravestone]

LAWSON, JAMES, born 1743, a farmer from Perthshire, with his wife Isabella born 1745, son John born 1782, son James born 1785, and daughter Eliza born 1792, emigrated via Port Glasgow aboard the Commerce bound for Pictou, Nova Scotia, on 10 August 1803. [NLS.ms1053.104-109]

LAWSON, THOMAS, born 1850, son of Robert Lawson, [1818-1899], a joiner, and his wife Jane McKenzie, [1822-1888], died in San Antonio, Texas, on 2 May 1883. [Coupar Angus gravestone]

LAYTON, DAVID STARK, born 1813, son of Thomas Layton, surgeon and medical superintendent on the Isle of Maintowanig, Upper Canada, died 25 October 1866. [Kinross, Kirkgate, gravestone]

LEGGET, WILLIAM, born 1781, died in Albany, New York, on 1 April 1832. [Perth gravestone]

LENNOX, JOHN, son of David Lennox a currier in Perth, was apprenticed to Thomas Hay Marshall a merchant in Perth in 1803. [PKA.B59.29.94]

LESLIE, JAMES, born 1748 in Dunkeld, died in Shelburne, Nova Scotia, on 15 September 1822. [Acadian Recorder, 28.9.1822]

LESLIE, JOHN, in Dunkeld, letters, 1823. [NRS.GD132.739]

LESLIE, JOHN, born 1835, son of John Leslie, [1805-1855], farmer at Easter Logie, and his wife Elspeth Webster, [1813-1908], died in America on 22 June 1878. [Dunkeld Cathedral gravestone]

LESLIE, WILLIAM, a blacksmith in Kincaidston Meadow, Caputh, accused of assault in 1824. [NRS.AD14.24.73]

LETHAME, JOHN, a shoemaker in Perth, testament, 1791, Comm. St Andrews. [NRS]

LIDDLE, ALEXANDER, a lime merchant in Perth, business correspondence, 1812. [NRS.B59.37.3.2]

LILLBURN, WALTER, of Birnyhill, Arngask, testament, 1793, Comm. St Andrews. [NRS]

LINDSAY, ALEXANDER, a tenant in the Myres of Errol, a bond of caution for John Dorward a tenant at the Mill of Myre, 1803. [NRS.CS271.531]

LINDSAY, ANN, born 1779, wife of Patrick Glenday, [1777-1836], died in St Charles, Missouri, on 3 November 1821. [Rattray gravestone]

LINDSAY, JAMES, [1829-1881], and his wife Margaret Steven, [1827-1889], parents of Elizabeth Lindsay, born 1870, died in Willoughby, Ohio, on 20 December 1915. [Abernyte gravestone]

LINDSAY, SAMUEL, a brewer in Dunkeld, versus David Freer, 1816. [NRS.CS40.22.166]

LINDSAY, WILLIAM, a carrier in Perth, was accused of forgery in 1832. [NRS.AD14.32.18]

LISTON, ANDREW, born 1777 in Perthshire, a millwright in St John, Colleton County, S.C., was naturalised in South Carolina on 16 November 1813. [NARA.M1183.1]

LISTON, HENRY, son of Reverend William Liston in Redgorton, was educated at Marischal College in 1850s, later a coffee planter in Ceylon, afterwards in Manitoba, Canada. [MCA]

LISTON, JAMES, son of James Liston, [died 1853], and his wife Isobel Soutar. [died 1863], died in Montreal, Quebec, on 8 January 1867. [Lethendy gravestone]

LIVINGSTONE, DONALD, with his wife Janet and three children, from Dull, emigrated via Greenock aboard the Curlew bound for Quebec on 21 July 1818. [TNA.CO384/3.123-127]

LOW, DAVID, son of James Low a smith in Kinross, was apprenticed to David Drysdale a saddle and harness maker in Perth in 1805. [NRS.GD1.427.16/9]

LOWE, DAVID, born 15 June 1828, son of John Lowe, [1801-1886], a surgeon in Coupar Angus, and his wife Marjory Clark, [1789-1877], died in Oregon, on 29 September 1858. [Coupar Angus Abbey gravestone]

LOW, ELIZABETH, in Dunning, was murdered in 1818. [NRS.AD14.18,248]

LOWE, GEORGE, born 18 April 1819, son of John Lowe, [1801-1886], a surgeon in Coupar Angus, and his wife Marjory Clark, [1789-1877], died in Buffalo, USA, on 2 February 1879. [Coupar Angus Abbey gravestone]

LOWE, JAMES, born 12 April 1830, son of John Lowe, [1801-1886], a surgeon in Coupar Angus, and his wife Marjory Clark, [1789-1877], died in San Francisco, California, on 2 February 1879. [Coupar Angus Abbey gravestone]

LOWE, JAMES MILLER, born 1830 in Perthshire, a minister in Thornton, Fife, died in Philadelphia, Pennsylvania, on 20 October 1872. [S.9150]

LOW, JOHN, of Brackly, Portmoak, Kinross, testament, 1795, Comm. St Andrews. [NRS]

LOWDEN, ELIZABETH, wife of Alexander Wilson a carter, was accused of forgery in Blairgowrie in 1824. [NRS.AD14.24.101]

LOWDEN, JAMES, a shoemaker in Doune, Kilmadock, was accused of hamesucken, assault, and theft in 1818. [NRS.AD14.18.88]

LOWSON, ANN BANNERMAN, daughter of George Lowson and his wife Catherine Paton, died in New Plymouth, New Zealand, on 23 November 1860. [Fowlis Easter gravestone]

LUMSDANE, GEORGE, born 1789, a labourer from Callander, emigrated via Port Glasgow aboard the Favourite of St John bound for St John, New Brunswick, on 22 October 1815. [PANB.ms.RS23E.fo.9798]

LUNDIE, W. H., a teacher in Auchterarder, father of Reverend Marshall Lundie, BD, born 1857, died at Tharais Mines, Calamas, Spain, on 4 December 1884. [S.12919]

LUNN, AGNES, born 1790 in Campsie, died on 18 October 1878. [St George gravestone, Port Elizabeth, South Africa]

MCALPIN, ALPINE, in Killin, was accused of poaching in 1801. [NRS.GD112.11.7.4.16]

MCANDREW, MILES, born 1807, a sailor found guilty of forgery, was sentenced at Perth to transportation to the colonies on 17 September 1832. [PKA.B59.26.11]

MCANSH, ALEXANDER, in Doune, 1818, a partner in the Allan Flax Spinning Company. [NRS.CS96.3561]

MACARA, ANDREW, born 1756 in Scotland, died at Rogers Hill, Nova Scotia, on 7 March 1832. [Halifax Journal, 26.3.1832]

MACARA, GEORGE, born 1800 in Perth, died in St John, New Brunswick, on 22 November 1828. [New Brunswick Courier, 22.11.1828]

MACARA, JANE, youngest daughter of Reverend John MacAra in Perthshire, married James Humphrey in Halifax, Nova Scotia, on 30 May 1830. [Acadian Recorder, 3.6.1830]

MCARA, ROBERT, born 1839, son of Robert McAra and his wife Christina McCulloch, died on 4 April 1871, and was buried in Warwick Cemetery, Queensland, Australia. [Monzie gravestone]

MACARA, WILLIAM, born 1791 in Perthshire, a druggist, died in Halifax, Nova Scotia, on 30 December 1835. [New Brunswick Royal Gazette, 13.1.1836]

MCARA, WILLIAM, born 1810, son of Charles McAra and his wife Jean Greig, died in New Zealand in 1864. [Monzie gravestone]

MCARDLE, DUNCAN, born 1782, a labourer from Dalvrack, Monzievaird, Perthshire, emigrated via Greenock aboard the William of New York bound for New York, landed there on 17 October 1817. [NY Municipal Archives][NY Commercial Advertiser, 18.10.1817]

MCARTHUR, ARTHUR, born 1785 in Perthshire, died in Sussex Vale, New Brunswick, on 1 March 1836. [NBC.12. 3.1836]

MCARTHUR, CATHERINE, with two children, from Comrie, emigrated via Greenock aboard the Curlew bound for Quebec on 21 July 1818. [TNA.CO384/3.123-127]

MCARTHUR, JAMES, with his wife Ann and five children, from Comrie, emigrated via Greenock aboard the Curlew bound for Quebec on 21 July 1818. [TNA.CO384/3.123-127]

MCARTHUR, JOHN, born 1745 in Perth, settled in Livingston, Maine, died in 1816. [Imm. New England.118]

MCARTHUR, ROBERT, a dyer in Callendar, died 13 September 1832. [NRS.S/H.1873]

MCBEATH, FINLAY, born 1823, son of Alexander McBeath and his wife Marjory McGregor, died in Glendaruel, Victoria, Australia, on 7 July 1860. [Blair Atholl gravestone]

MCCALL, JAMES, born 1830, son of John McCall and his wife Janet Steven, died in Melbourne, Victoria, Australia, on 26 August 1867. [Muthill gravestone]

MCCALL, W. F., from Aberfeldy, died at the residence of his uncle D. McGregor in Houston, Texas, on 26 September 1873, [S.9447]

MCCALLUM, DUNCAN, born 1794, a labourer from Aberfoyle, emigrated via Port Glasgow aboard the Favourite of St John bound for St John, New Brunswick, on 22 October 1815. [PANB.ms.RS23E.fo.9798]

MCCALLUM, DUNCAN, with his wife Christine and one child, from Comrie, emigrated via Greenock aboard the Curlew bound for Quebec on 21 July 1818. [TNA.CO384/3.123-127]

MCCALLUM, DUNCAN, with two children, from Comrie, emigrated via Greenock aboard the Curlew bound for Quebec on 21 July 1818. [TNA.CO384/3.123-127]

MCCALLUM, DUNCAN, born 1862, son of ......McCallum and his wife Mary Robertson, died in Brisbane, Queensland, Australia, in June 1881. [New Scone gravestone]

MCCALLUM, JOHN, born 1791, a labourer from Gartmore, emigrated via Port Glasgow aboard the Favourite of St John bound for St John, New Brunswick, on 22 October 1815. [PANB.ms.RS23E.fo.9798]

MCCALLUM, MARGARET, in Margowan, Killin, a petition to the Earl of Breadalbane in 1802. [NRS.GD112.11.7.5.28]

MCCALLUM, PETER, from Clunie, emigrated to North America via Liverpool in June 1833. [SG.2.152]

MCCALLUM, PETER, born 1837, an architect from Perth, died in St Louis, Missouri, on 8 May 1887. [FFP]

MCCONNELL, DANIEL, of 1 Lickley Street, Perth, father of Daniel McConnell, born 1866, died in St Paul, Minnesota, on 28 January 1891. [Perthshire Weekly News.1866]

MCCORQUODALE, JOHN, in Scone, applied to be land steward at Taymouth in 1843. [NRS.GD112.11.10.8A.37]

MCCOWAN, DUNCAN, with two children, from Comrie, emigrated via Greenock aboard the Curlew bound for Quebec on 21 July 1818. [TNA.CO384/3.123-127]

MCCOWAN, JAMES, with his wife Janet, from Comrie, emigrated via Greenock aboard the Curlew bound for Quebec on 21 July 1818. [TNA.CO384/3.123-127]

MCCOWAN, WILLIAM, born 1817, a soldier of the 58th Massachusetts Infantry, died at Camp Readville, USA, on 1 April 1864. [Dunblane gravestone]

MCCRAW, DONALD, born 1736, a merchant in Kirkgate Street, Perth, found guilty of murder and sentenced to death by hanging in Perth on 11 July 1806. [NRS.JC11.48]

MCCULLOCH, DONALD, in Hammerhaugh, Little Dunkeld, a victim of theft in 1830. [NRS.AD14.30.21]

MCCULLOM, WILLIAM, born 1778 in Perth, a mariner who died in Savanna, Georgia, on 6 December 1806. [Savanna Death Register]

MCDERMID, ARCHIBALD, probably from Perthshire, settled in Reach, Canada West by 1848. [NRS.GD112.61.5/2]

MCDERMID, COLIN, probably from Perthshire, settled in Reach, Canada West by 1848. [NRS.GD112.61.5/2]

MCDERMID, JOHN, probably from Perthshire, settled in Reach, Canada West by 1848. [NRS.GD112.61.5/2]

MCDIARMID, ARCHIBALD, with his wife Mary and two children, from Killin, emigrated via Greenock aboard the Curlew bound for Quebec on 21 July 1818. [TNA.CO384/3.123-127]

MCDIARMID, DUNCAN, with his wife Mary and two children, from Comrie, emigrated via Greenock aboard the Curlew bound for Quebec on 21 July 1818. [TNA.CO384/3.123-127]

MACDIARMID, ELIZA, only daughter of Duncan MacDiarmid in Kynachan, married James Ferguson from Hanover, Jamaica, at Dunfallandie in 1809. [EA.XCI.4733]

MCDIARMID, HUGH, with his wife Janet and two children, from Dull, emigrated via Greenock aboard the Curlew bound for Quebec on 21 July 1818. [TNA.CO384/3.123-127]

MCDIARMID, Reverend JAMES, in Weem, a letter, 1808. [NRS.GD170.2956]

MCDIARMID, JOHN, born 1791, a labourer from Kenmore, with his wife Isabella born 1788, emigrated via Port Glasgow aboard the Favourite of St John bound for St John, New Brunswick, on 22 October 1815. [PANB.ms.RS23E.fo.9798]

MCDIARMID, JOHN, a shepherd in Milnathort, Kinross, was accused of sheep stealing in 1847. [NRS.AD14.47.200]

MCDONALD, ALEXANDER, a saddler in Dunkeld, and Alexander McLean, a saddler in Dunkeld, a contract of co-partnership dated 1835. [PKA.B59.38.6.277]

MCDONALD, ALEXANDER, a banker in Callander, a petition in 1814. [NRS.CC2.7.62.5]

MCDONALD, ALEXANDER, in Aberfeldy, a victim of forgery in 1835. [NRS.AD14.35.80]

MCDONALD, ALEXANDER, in Kindrogie, Moulin, a victim of assault in 1845. [NRS.AD14.45.291]

MCDONALD, ALEXANDER, in Rinegour by Aberfoyle, a victim of forgery in 1851. [NRS.AD14.51.522]

MCDONALD, ALLAN, in Wester Aberfeldy, a petition concerning his son a cabinet maker in London, 1821. [NRS.GD112.11.8.13.32]

MCDONALD, ALLAN, born 1819, a thief who was sentenced in Perth to transportation to the colonies on 17 September 1832. [PKA.B59.26.11]

MCDONALD, ARCHIBALD, a farmer in Balquhidder, a petition in 1801. [NRS.GD112.11.7.4.11]

MCDONALD, BARBARA, in Perth, found guilty of stealing sheep was sentenced to transportation to the colonies for seven years in 1802. [PKA.B59.26.11.2]

MCDONALD, CHARLES, born 1768, a farmer from Perthshire, with his wife Agnes born 1772, daughter Eliza born 1794, son Alexander born 1801, and son James born 1802, emigrated via Port Glasgow aboard the Commerce bound for Pictou, Nova Scotia, on 10 August 1803. [NLS.ms1053.104-109]

MCDONALD, CHARLES, born 1761, from Moulin, emigrated to Canada in 1803, died at Scotch Hill, Nova Scotia, on 8 February 1842. [Halifax Journal, 21.3.1842]

MCDONALD, CHARLES, born 1789, a confectioner and broker, 143 South Street, Perth, was accused of uttering forged and base coin in Doune in 1832. [NRS.AD14.32.139]; found guilty and sentenced to transportation to the colonies for seven years in April 1832. [PKA.B59.26.11.3.6]

MCDONALD, CHRISTINE, found guilty of theft was sentenced to transportation to the colonies, in Perth on 19 April 1833. [PKA.B59.26.11]

MCDONALD, DONALD, born 1781, a labourer from Foss, with his wife Margaret born 1786, and daughter Elizabeth born 1807, emigrated aboard the Clarendon of Hull bound for Prince Edward Island in August 1808. [NSARM] [TNA.CO226.23]

MCDONALD, DONALD, born in Drumcastle, Rannoch, was educated at the University of St Andrews, a minister in Canada from 1824, died at Orwell Head, Prince Edward Island, on 21 February 1867. [F.7.621]

MCDONALD, DONALD, born 1841, died in Brisbane, Queensland, Australia, on 2 December 1868. [Balquhidder gravestone]

MCDONALD, FINLAY, born 1781 in Logerait, son of Donald MacDonald and his wife Christine Stewart, emigrated to Prince Edward Island around 1825. ['Skye Pioneers and the Island'.83]

MACDONALD, HUGH, from Perthshire, settled at Lime Rock, West River, Nova Scotia, died 16 November 1866, husband of Margaret, ......, born 1809, died 1897. [Caledonia gravestone, Pictou, NS]

MCDONALD, JAMES, born 1771, a labourer from Atholl, with his wife Isobel born 1773, son Donald born 1798, Margaret born 1800, Elizabeth born 1804, and son John born 1806, emigrated aboard the Clarendon of Hull bound for Prince Edward Island in August 1808. [NSARM] [TNA.CO226.23]

MCDONALD, JAMES, son of James McDonald a farmer in Logie Almond, a student at Marischal College, Aberdeen in 1840s. [MCA]

MCDONALD, JANET, born 1807 in Dunblane, a handloom weaver, was accused of forgery in 1831. [NRS.AD14.31.249]

MCDONALD, JANET, in Wester Aberfeldy, widow of Duncan McPherson, a petition, 1824. [NRS.GD112.11.118.16.21]

MCDONALD, JOHN, in Aberfeldy, a sequestration petition, 1849. [NRS.CS279.1852]

MCDONALD, JOHN, in Craighead of Persey, Bendochy, a victim of theft in 1837. [NRS.AD14.37.141]

MCDONALD, MARGARET, born 1794 in Dunkeld, wife of Thomas Edmondson in Shettleston, Glasgow, was accused of forgery in 1831. [NRS.AD14.31.360]

MCDONALD, PETER, son of Alexander McDonald, a flax draper in Blairgowrie, was accused of housebreaking in 1827. [NRS.AD14.27.197]

MCDONALD, WILLIAM, a sheep dealer in Croft Blackcraig, accused of sheep stealing in 1825. [NRS.JC26.1825.295]

MCDOUGALD, PETER, born 1791 in Perthshire, emigrated to New Brunswick in 1821, died at Salt Springs, Upham parish, King's County, N.B. [New Brunswick Courier.3.4.1841]

MCDOUGALL, ALLAN, son of Hugh McDougall, [1786-1852], a farmer, and his wife Janet McDougall, [1792-1876], emigrated to Australia. [Fortingall gravestone]

MCDOUGALL, JOHN, born 1827, eldest son of Hugh McDougall a farmer in Kinghalin, Fortingall, died at Bridgewater-on-Lodden, Victoria, Australia, on 27 June 1884. [S.12833]

MACDOUGALL, ROBERT, from Perthshire to Goderich, Upper Canada, in 1836, [Author of The Emigrant's Guide to North America, 1841]

MCEWAN, DAVID, of Deanston village, Kilmadock, was murdered in 1846. [NRS.JC26.1846.33]

MCEWAN, DUNCAN, a joiner in Callendar, was accused of assault, found guilty and sentenced to six months imprisonment in 1819. [NRS.JC11.60]

MCEWAN, DUNCAN, born 1818, son of Hugh McEwan, [1785-1834], a mason in Dunkeld, and his wife Christian McCullum, [1783-1861], died in Detroit, Michigan on 27 July 1856. [Little Dunkeld gravestone]

MCEWEN, EWEN, son of Alexander McEwen, [1715-1797], a farmer in Keprannich, and his wife Janet McVichie, [1736-1794], settled in New York, died in Newtown, Killin, on 21 September 1811. [Kenmore Ardtainaig gravestone]

MCEWAN, ELIZABETH, mother of Peter, John, and Janet, in Cromlix, a victim of housebreaking and theft in 1835. [NRS.AD14.35.108]

MCEWEN, FINLAY, with his wife Mary and seven children, from Balquhidder, emigrated via Greenock aboard the Sophia of Ayr bound for Quebec on 26 July 1818. [TNA.CO384/3.133-134]

MCEWAN, JANET, in Cromlix, a victim of housebreaking and theft in 1835. [NRS.AD14.35.108]

MCEWEN, JOHN, with his wife Catherine and two children, from Little Dunkeld, emigrated via Greenock aboard the Curlew bound for Quebec on 21 July 1818. [TNA.CO384/3.123-127]

MCEWEN, JOHN, with one child, from Comrie, emigrated via Greenock aboard the Curlew bound for Quebec on 21 July 1818. [TNA.CO384/3.123-127]

MCEWAN, JOHN, born 1806, son of William McEwan, [1768-1832], died in Mexico in 1832. [Logerait gravestone]

MCEWAN, JOHN, in Cromlix, a victim of housebreaking and theft in 1835. [NRS.AD14.35.108]

MCEWAN, MARGARET, born 11 September 1811, wife of Daniel McIldowie, died in Dunedin, New Zealand, on 2 July 1885. [Monzievaird gravestone]

MCEWAN, PETER, in Cromlix, a victim of housebreaking and theft in 1835. [NRS.AD14.35.108]

MCEWAN, WILLIAM, with one child, from Comrie, emigrated via Greenock aboard the Curlew bound for Quebec on 21 July 1818. [TNA.CO384/3.123-127]

MCFARLAND, PETER, and his three wives, 1781. [Logerait gravestone]

MCFARLANE, ALEXANDER, born 1790, a labourer from Callendar, emigrated via Port Glasgow aboard the Favourite of St John bound for St John, New Brunswick, on 22 October 1815. [PANB.ms.RS23E.fo.9798]

MCFARLANE, ALEXANDER, with his wife and four children, from Blackhills, Perthshire, emigrated via Liverpool to North America in June 1833. [SG.2.152]

MCFARLANE, ALEXANDER, in Blairgowrie, a sequestration petition, 1849. [NRS.CS279.1903]

MACFARLANE, DANIEL, born 1784 in Glen Dochart, emigrated to Nova Scotia in 1806, died 13 November 1849, husband of Helen MacNab, born 1795, died 1849. [Wallace gravestone, Cumberland County, NS]

MCFARLANE, DONALD, born 1752, tenant of Little Findowie, Dunkeld, was accused of assaulting, stabbing, and wounding, in 1828. [NRS.AD14.28.256]

MCFARLANE, DUNCAN, born 1782 in Aberfoyle, a grocer in Halifax, Nova Scotia, died there on 17 April 1842, probate 1842, Halifax, N.S. [Acadian Recorder, 23.4.1842]

MCFARLANE, DUNCAN, born 1782, a labourer from Strathfillan, emigrated via Port Glasgow aboard the <u>Favourite of St John</u> bound for St John, New Brunswick, on 22 October 1815. [PANB.ms.RS23E.fo.9798]

MCFARLANE, DUNCAN, born 1810, from Port of Menteith, died at the Karn Melks River, Caledon, South Africa, on 25 July 1884. [S.12838]

MCFARLANE, FEMIE, from Kincarnie, Clunie, Perthshire, emigrated via Liverpool to North America in 1833. [SG.II.152]

MACFARLANE, JAMES, born 1811, son of Alexander MacFarlane, [1763-1838], an iron-founder in Perth, and his wife Euphemia Watson, [1778-1854], died 1856 in Chicago, Illinois. [Perth, Greyfriars, gravestone]

MACFARLANE, JOHN, born 1747 in Perthshire, died in Wallace, Nova Scotia, on 2 August 1841. [Halifax Journal, 16.8.1841]

MCFARLANE, JOHN, born 1762, a farmer from Perthshire, with his wife Ann born 1764, daughter Eliza born 1793, son James born 1795, son John born 1797, daughter Ann born 1799, daughter Margaret born 1801, and Janet born 1803, emigrated via Port Glasgow aboard the <u>Commerce</u> bound for Pictou, Nova Scotia, on 10 August 1803. [NLS.ms1053.104-109]

MCFARLANE, JOHN, a carrier in Killin, applied for the pendicle of Finlay Campbell a shoemaker there in 1802. [NRS.GD112.11.7.5.6]

MCFARLANE, JOHN, a labourer in Dunkeld, was accused of sheep stealing in 1819. [NRS.AD14.19.180]

MCFARLANE, JOHN, with his family from Clunie, Perthshire, emigrated via Liverpool to North America in 1833. [SG.II.152]

MCFARLANE, JOHN, an auctioneer in Burrelton, Cargill, was accused of forgery in 1834. [NRS.AD14.34.412]

MCFARLANE, MALCOLM, born 1786 in Perthshire, a merchant in Charleston, South Carolina, was naturalised on 23 October 1813. [NARA.M1183.1]

MCFARLAN, MARGARET, born 1763 in Perthshire, died 7 March 1833, wife of Alexander Stewart. [North Lochaber cemetery, Antigonish County, NS]

MCFARLANE, or DRUMMOND, MARY, a weaver in Dunning, was accused of theft in 1818. [NRS.AD14.18.31]

MCFARLANE, MUNGO, born 1780, a labourer from Strathbraan, emigrated aboard the Clarendon of Hull bound for Prince Edward Island in August 1808. [NSARM] [TNA.CO226.23]

MACFARLANE, NORMAN, born 1846, son of William MacFarlane, a clothier in Coupar Angus, and his wife Elizabeth Will, died in Chicago, Illinois, on 21 March 1892. [Coupar Angus gravestone]

MCFARLANE, PARLANE, a blacksmith and farrier in Perth, 1804. [NRS.GD1.427.16/7]

MCFARLANE, PETER, born 1783, a labourer from Caplia, with his wife Janet, born 1783, emigrated aboard the Clarendon of Hull bound for Prince Edward Island in August 1808. [NSARM] [TNA.CO226.23]

MCFARLANE, PETER, born 1819 in Perth, son of Alexander McFarlane, an iron founder, and his wife Euphemia Watson, [1778-1854], died in Montreal, Quebec, in 1879. [Perth, Greyfriars, gravestone]

MCFARLANE, WALTER, son of John McFarlane a quarrier in Inchewan, Little Dunkeld, 1833. [NRS.AC14.33.7]

MCFARLANE, Dr WILLIAM, a physician in Dunkeld, a victim of assault in 1821. [NRS.AD14.21.89]

MCFARLANE, WILLIAM STEWART, born December 1814 in Perth, son of Alexander McFarlane, an iron founder, and his wife Euphemia Watson, [1778-1854], died in Montreal, Quebec, in February 1885. [Perth, Greyfriars, gravestone]

MCFARLANE, WILLIAM, son of William McFarlane in Little Findowie, Dunkeld, was accused of assaulting, stabbing, and wounding, in 1828. [NRS.AD14.28.256]

MCGIBBON, DONALD, a weaver, and former soldier of the 1st Battalion of the Breadalbane Fencibles, applied for property in Ballechroisk in 1802. [NRS.GD112.11.7.5.15]

MCGIBBON, Mrs FRANCES, wife of John McGibbon, late of Newfoundland, died in Killin on 5 November 1847. [Lawers gravestone]

MCGIBBON, JOHN, a carpenter in St George, New Brunswick, later in Trelawney, Jamaica, son of Duncan McGibbon, [1727-1812], and his wife Margaret Campbell, [1737-1807], in Glen Quaich, died at sea between Jamaica and Nova Scotia, probate 7 May 1787, New Brunswick. [Amulree gravestone]

MCGIBBON, JOHN, a merchant in St John's, Newfoundland, later in Killin, died by 1853. [NRS.CS280.39.146]

MCGIBBON, JOSEPH, son of Duncan McGibbon, [1727-1812], and his wife Margaret Campbell, [1737-1807], died at sea between Jamaica and Nova Scotia. [Amulree gravestone]

MCGIBBON, MALCOLM, in Killin, was murdered in 1831. [NRS.A14.31.70]

MCGIBBON, PATRICK, son of Duncan McGibbon, [1727-1812], and his wife Margaret Campbell, [1737-1807], died at sea between Jamaica and Nova Scotia. [Amulree gravestone]

MCGILLEVRIE, JOHN, born 1791, son of Peter McGillevrie, a farmer, [1755-1830]. And his wife Janet Robertson, [1768-1838], died in Richmond, Virginia, in 1820. [Logerait gravestone]

MCGLASHAN, JAMES, born 1797 in Perthshire, a cooper, died 8 September 1837 in St John, New Brunswick. [NBC.9.9.1837]

MCGLASHAN, JAMES, in Strathbraan, dead by 1855. [NRS.S/H]

MCGLASHAN, JOHN, born 1819, son of Mary Pullar or McGlashan a widow in Wester Inchewan, Little Dunkeld, 1833. [NRS.AC14.33.7]

MCGLASHAN, PATRICK, in Tynereach, Moulinean, formerly a sawmiller at Blair Atholl, was accused of assault in 1832. [NRS.AD14.32.8]

MCGREGOR, ALEXANDER, in Kintillo, Dunbarnie, testament, 1793, Comm. St Andrews. [NRS]

MCGREGOR, ALEXANDER, minister in Balquhidder, a letter, 1825. [NRS.GD112.74.693.5/6]

MCGREGOR, ALEXANDER, born 1743, a farmer from Perthshire, with Margaret McDonald born 1763, emigrated via Port Glasgow aboard the Commerce bound for Pictou, Nova Scotia, on 10 August 1803. [NLS.ms1053.104-109]

MCGREGOR, ALEXANDER, with his wife Mary and one child, from Balquhidder, emigrated via Greenock aboard the Sophia of Ayr bound for Quebec on 26 July 1818. [TNA.CO384/3.133-134]

MCGREGOR, ALEXANDER, with his wife Janet and three children, from Callander, emigrated via Greenock aboard the Curlew bound for Quebec on 21 July 1818. [TNA.CO384/3.123-127]

MCGREGOR, ALEXANDER, a carrier between Perth and Aberfeldy, 1819. [NRS.CS36.27.94]

MCGREGOR, ALEXANDER, in Ruthvenfield, Tibbermuir, a victim of embezzlement in 1849. [NRS.AD14.49.93]

MCGREGOR, ALEXANDER, [1839-1929], and his wife Grace Duff, [1854-1911], parents of Mary McGregor, born 1876, died in Detroit, Michigan, on 9 May 1928. [Aberfeldy gravestone]

MCGREGOR, ALPINE, born 1746, late of the Braes of Moness, now in Aberfeldy, applied to be rent free, in 1831. [NRS.GD112.11.9.7.80]

MCGREGOR, Mrs ANN, born 1794 in Perthshire, died 12 January 1839, wife of John McGregor. [Anglican cemetery, Halifax County, NS]

MCGREGOR, ANN, in Perth Tolbooth, accused of theft in 1816. [NRS.JC26.1816.139]

MCGREGOR, ARCHIBALD, born 1780, a labourer from Appin Menzies, with his wife Christian, born 1784, and son Alexander born 1805, emigrated aboard the Clarendon of Hull bound for Prince Edward Island, Canada, in August 1808. [NSARM] [TNA.CO226.23]

MCGREGOR, ARCHIBALD, with his wife Janet and two children, from Balquhidder, emigrated via Greenock aboard the Sophia of Ayr bound for Quebec on 26 July 1818. [TNA.CO384/3.133-134]

MCGREGOR, CATHERINE, youngest daughter of Rob Roy McGregor in Foss, married Duncan Campbell of Rosario de Santa Fe, late of Killin, at 334 Calle St Martin, Buenos Ayres, in 1868. [S.7872]

MCGREGOR, CHARLES, in Milton of Edradour, Moulin, the victim of an assault in 1832. [NRS.AD14.32.8]

MCGREGOR, CHARLES, in Ballintuim, a sequestration petition, 1849. [NRS.CS279.1781]

MCGREGOR, CHRISTINE, widow of Daniel McAlpine, High Street, Perth, a prisoner in Perth Tolbooth, found guilty of theft, was sentenced to fourteen years transportation to the colonies, in 1819. [NRS.JC26.1819.85]

MCGREGOR, COLIN, in Blairgowrie, a sequestration petition, 1849. [NRS.CS279.1781]

MCGREGOR, DAVID, in Kenmore, married Mary Johnstone Cumming, only daughter of William Cumming, at Prospect Hill Mountain, Canada West, on 17 February 1859. [CM.21660]

MCGREGOR, DAVID, born 1850, son of John McGregor and his wife Mary Geddes, died in Hamilton, Canada, on 26 March 1889. [Perth, Greyfriars, gravestone]

MCGREGOR, DONALD, in Perth, testament, 1793, Comm. St Andrews. [NRS]

MCGREGOR, DONALD, born 1781, a labourer from Callendar, emigrated via Port Glasgow aboard the Favourite of St John bound for St John, New Brunswick, on 22 October 1815. [PANB.ms.RS23E.fo.9798]

MCGREGOR, DONALD, a labourer in Kinross, was accused of housebreaking and theft in 1834. [NRS.AD14.34.317]

MCGREGOR, DONALD, of Balhaldie, died 30 December 1854, [NRS.S/H]

MCGREGOR, DOUGAL, born 1842, son of Alexander McGregor and his wife Jane Comrie, died in July 1893 in Croydon, Queensland. [Callander gravestone]

MCGREGOR, DUNCAN, born 1762, a farmer from Perthshire, with his wife Margaret born 1773, daughter Katherine born 1795, son Charles born 1797, son Hugh born 1799, and daughter Jessie born 1802, emigrated via Port Glasgow aboard the Commerce bound for Pictou, Nova Scotia, on 10 August 1803. [NLS.ms1053, fos.104-109]

MCGREGOR, DUNCAN, born 1773 in Perthshire, died in November 1829 in King's County, New Brunswick. [New Brunswick Courier, 28.11.1829]

MCGREGOR, DUNCAN, born 1775, a labourer from Callendar, with his wife Janet born 1776, and children Catherine born 1795, Margaret born 1797 a servant, Gregor born 1798 a labourer, Isabella born 1800 servant, Mary born 1801, Marjorie born 1803, James born 1809, and Elizabeth born 1809, emigrated via Port Glasgow aboard the Favourite of St John bound for St John, New Brunswick, on 22 October 1815. [PANB.ms.RS23E.fo.9798]

MCGREGOR, Sir E. J. MURRAY, of Lenric, born 1785, Governor and Commander in Chief in Barbados, St Vincent, Grenada, Tobago, St Lucia and Trinidad, died in Barbados on 14 June 1841. [GM.NS16.540]

MCGREGOR, EWAN MURRAY, in Kilmadock, a victim of housebreaking in 1835. [NRS.AD14.35.115]

MCGREGOR, GREGOR, in Callander, was accused of stabbing, 1814. [NRS.AD14.44.33]

MCGREGOR, HUGH, a journeyman shoemaker in Dune, Kilmadock, accused of housebreaking, theft and prison breaking in 1839. [NRS.AD14.39.61]

MCGREGOR, HUGH, born 1789 in Perthshire, the Customs Collector at Dickenson's Landing, died in Kingston, Upper Canada, on 16 May 1847. [AJ.5189]

MCGREGOR, ISABELLA, born 1 November 1830 in Crieff, daughter of James McGregor, [1787-1837], and his wife Margaret Ferguson, [1793-1842], died in Cleveland, Ohio, on 4 January 1891. [Tillicoutry gravestone]

MCGREGOR, JAMES, born 1765 in Perthshire, died at Loch Lomond, St John County, New Brunswick, on 21 May 1832. [New Brunswick Courier, 26.5.1832]

MCGREGOR, JAMES, born 1775, a labourer from Strathyre, Balquhidder, with his wife Margaret born 1777, and children Elizabeth born 1800, Janet born 1802, William born 1804, Colin born 1805, John born 1812, and James born 1813, emigrated via Port Glasgow aboard the Favourite of St John bound for St John, New Brunswick, on 22 October 1815. [PANB.ms.RS23E.fo.9798]

MCGREGOR, JAMES, born 1800, a labourer from Callendar, emigrated via Port Glasgow aboard the Favourite of St John bound for St John, New Brunswick, on 22 October 1815. [PANB.ms.RS23E.fo.9798]

MCGREGOR, JAMES, born 1814, son of John McGregor, a vintner in Perth, and his wife Catherine McDonald, died at Barker's Creek, Victoria, Australia, on 30 October 1847. [Greyfriars graveyard, Perth]

MCGREGOR, JAMES, a labourer in Rattray, accused of theft in 1828. [NRS.AD14.28.247]

MCGREGOR, JOHN, born 1786, a labourer from Strathgarry, emigrated aboard the Clarendon of Hull bound for Prince Edward Island, Canada, in August 1808. [NSARM] [TNA.CO226.23]

MCGREGOR, JOHN, born 1794, a labourer from Callendar, emigrated via Port Glasgow aboard the Favourite of St John bound for St John, New Brunswick, on 22 October 1815. [PANB.ms.RS23E.fo.9798]

MCGREGOR, JOHN, from Comrie, emigrated via Greenock aboard the Curlew bound for Quebec on 21 July 1818. [TNA.CO384/3.123-127]

MCGREGOR, JOHN, born 1796, a labourer from Aberfeldy, emigrated aboard the Clarendon of Hull bound for Prince Edward Island, Canada, in August 1808. [TNA.CO226.23][NSARM]

MCGREGOR, JOHN, born 1 December 1797 in Dull, son of Thomas McGregor and his wife Margaret McLaren, emigrated via Oban to Charlottetown, Prince Edward Island on 6 October 1808, settled in Nacagdoches, Texas, a piper, sergeant and cannoneer, fought at the Battle of Bexar in December 1835, died at the Alamo, Texas, on 6 March 1836. [Sgen.39.2.84] [DRTL][Dull OPR]

MCGREGOR, JOHN, with his wife Catherine and one child, from Balquhidder, emigrated via Greenock aboard the Sophia of Ayr bound for Quebec on 26 July 1818. [TNA.CO384/3.133-134]

MCGREGOR, JOHN, born 10 October 1822 in Crieff, son of James McGregor, [1787-1837], and his wife Margaret Ferguson, [1793-1842], died in Newark, New Jersey, on 5 July 1890. [Tillicoutry gravestone]

MCGREGOR, KATHERINE, born 1 June 1826 in Crieff, daughter of James McGregor, [1787-1837], and his wife Margaret Ferguson, [1793-1842], died in Newark, New Jersey, on 5 December 1893. [Tillicoutry gravestone]

MCGREGOR, Mrs MARGARET, born 1776 in Perthshire, wife of James McGregor, died at Loch Lomond, New Brunswick, on 21 November 1831. [New Brunswick Courier. 26.11.1831]

MCGREGOR, MARGARET, born 15 September 1827 in Crieff, daughter of James McGregor, [1787-1837], and his wife Margaret Ferguson, [1793-1842], died in Cleveland, Ohio, on 31 August 1859, wife of Richard Huddleston. [Tillicoutry gravestone]

MCGREGOR, MARY, fifth daughter of the late Duncan McGregor from Perthshire, married Donald Gunn in St John, New Brunswick, on 31 May 1830. [New Brunswick Courier, 5.6.1830]

MCGREGOR, NEIL, born 1773 in Perthshire, a gardener in Charleston, South Carolina, was naturalised on 23 August 1813. [NARA.M1183.1]

MCGREGOR, PATRICK, a merchant in St Thomas in the East, Jamaica, son of Christian McDougall or McGregor in Dull, testament, 1823, Comm. Edinburgh. [NRS]

MCGREGOR, PETER, in Perth, testament, 1800, Comm. St Andrews. [NRS]

MCGREGOR, PETER, born 1791, a labourer from Callendar, with Peter McGregor, born 1813 in Callendar, emigrated via Port Glasgow aboard the Favourite of St John bound for St John, New Brunswick, on 22 October 1815. [PANB.ms.RS23E.fo.9798]

MCGREGOR, PETER, with his wife Catherine, and two children, from Balquhidder, emigrated via Greenock aboard the Sophia of Ayr bound for Quebec on 26 July 1818. [TNA.CO384/3.133-134]

MCGREGOR, PETER, with his wife Christine, from Comrie, emigrated via Greenock aboard the Curlew bound for Quebec on 21 July 1818. [TNA.CO384/3.123-127]

MCGREGOR, PETER, with his wife Mary, and two children, from Balquhidder, emigrated via Greenock aboard the Sophia of Ayr bound for Quebec on 26 July 1818. [TNA.CO384/3.133-134]

MCGREGOR, PETER, born 1822, son of Robert McGregor, a merchant in Kinloch, died in Melbourne, Australia, on 3 May 1879. [Fortingall Killochoman gravestone]

MCGREGOR, ROBERT, with his wife Mary and two children, from Comrie, emigrated via Greenock aboard the Curlew bound for Quebec on 21 July 1818. [TNA.CO384/3.123-127]

MCGREGOR, ROBERT KETTLE, born 1849, son of John McGregor and his wife Mary Geddes, died in Melbourne, Australia, on 2 January 1886. [Perth, Greyfriars gravestone]

MCGREGOR, THOMAS, born 1768, a labourer from Aberfeldy, emigrated aboard the Clarendon of Hull bound for Prince Edward Island, Canada, in August 1808. [NSARM] [TNA.CO226.23]

MCGREGOR, WILLIAM, in New Rattray, a sequestration petition, 1849. [NRS.CS279.1781]

MCGRIGOR, DONALD, a builder in Aberfeldy, petitioned for land there in 1808. [NRS.GD112.11.8.4.5]

MCGRIGOR, JOHN, in Aberfeldy, petitioned for land there in 1808. [NRS.GD112.11.8.4.5]

MCGRIGOR, ROBERT, a weaver in Stanley, dead by 1860, father of James McGrigor a commission agent in Cincinatti, Ohio. [NRS.S/H]

MCGRUTHER, JOHN, a writer in Dunblane, versus Charles Greig, a shipmaster in Kincardine, 1834. [NRS.CS46.1834.2.57]; versus John Dempster, a mason in Alloa, 1838. [NRS.CS46.1838.108]

MCGRUTHER, WILLIAM, son of John McGruther and his wife Janet Buchan, died in Melbourne, Australia, in August 1888. [Dunblane gravestone]

MCINNES, BENJAMIN, born 1812 in Perthshire, a smith in Charleston, South Carolina, who was naturalised there on 7 January 1847. [NARA.M1183.1]

MCINNES, JAMES, with his wife Marion and one child, from Callander, emigrated via Greenock aboard the Curlew bound for Quebec on 21 July 1818. [TNA.CO384/3.123-127]

MCINNES, JOHN, tenant farmer in Easter Miggar, Comrie, was accused of sheep stealing in 1801. [NRS.JC26.1801.48/6]

MCINNES, JOSEPH, born 6 April 1772 in Muthill, emigrated to Charleston, South Carolina, in 1800, died there on 25 July 1851. [Second Presbyterian gravestone, Charleston]

MCINNES, ROBERT, from Aberfoyle, died in Carriere, Grenada, in 1817. [S.43.17]

MCINNES, ROBERT, born 1812, a butcher in Dunblane, was accused of sheep stealing in 1833. [NRS.AD14.33.12]

MCINROY, DAVID, born 29 July 1831, third son of James Patrick McInroy of Lude and his wife Margaret Seton Lillie, died in San Jorge, Banda Oriental, Uruguay, on 23 March 1868. [Kilmonivaig gravestone, Blair Atholl]

MCINROY, HENRY, born 1841, son of James Patrick McInroy of Lude and his wife Margaret Seaton Lillie, died in Colorado on 12 June 1902. [Kilmaveonaig gravestone, Blair Atholl]

MCINROY, PATRICK, born 16 July 1845, youngest son of James Patrick McInroy of Lude and his wife Margaret Seaton Lillie, married Amelia Annie Curtis daughter of H. H. Curtis, at Oaklands Hall, Douglas County, Colorado, on 23 November 1872, died in Pueblo, Colorado, on 12 November 1882. [Kilmaveonaig gravestone, Blair Atholl] [S.9177]

MCINTOSH, ALEXANDER, born 1761, a farmer from Perthshire, with his wife Agnes born 1769, daughter Margaret born 1792, son James born 1794, and son William born 1800, emigrated via Port Glasgow aboard the Commerce bound for Pictou, Nova Scotia, on 10 August 1803. [NLS.ms1053.104-109]

MCINTOSH, DANIEL, a merchant in Killin, sederunt book, 1809-1810, [NRS.CS96.3358]

MCINTOSH, DONALD, born 1780 in Bannach, Atholl, born 1780, died 2 May 1842, husband of Christie Fraser, born 1804, died 7 July 1897. [Hill gravestone, Pictou, NS]

MCINTOSH, GILBERT, a dyer and weaver in Killin, was accused of assault in 1831. [NRS.AD14.31.47]

MCINTOSH, JOHN, in Kirkmichael, a victim of assault in 1845. [NRS.AD14.45.291]

MCINTYRE, Reverend ALEXANDER, in Kinloch Rannoch, 1845 -1849. [NRS.CH2.1298.39]

MCINTYRE, DONALD, with his wife Isabella, and two children, from Killin, emigrated via Greenock aboard the Sophia of Ayr bound for Quebec on 26 July 1818. [TNA.CO384/3.133-134]

MCINTYRE, DUNCAN, in Killin, applied for the farm of Ardnabuich in 1804. [NRS.GD112.11.7.7.30]

MCINTYRE, DUNCAN, son of William McIntyre a surgeon in Fortingall, graduated MA from Marischal College, Aberdeen, in 1844. [MCA]

MCINTYRE, DUNCAN, born 1825, son of Donald McIntyre and his wife Margaret Ferguson, died 1869 in Australia. [Callendar gravestone]

MCINTYRE, ELIZABETH MCLAREN, born 1807, daughter of Donald McIntyre, [1766-1856], a farmer in Wester Dundurcas, and his wife Margaret Ferguson, [1787-1875], died 1837 in Canada. [Comrie gravestone]

MCINTYRE, JAMES, a builder in Aberfeldy, petitioned for land there in 1808. [NRS.GD112.11.8.4.5]

MCINTYRE, JEAN, daughter of Alexander McIntyre, a labourer at Battlefield, Redgorton, and his wife Margaret Bain, accused of housebreaking and theft in 1822. [NRS.AD14.22.121]

MCINTYRE, JOHN, born in Glen Orchy in 1766, settled in Callander in 1814, charged with a firearm offence in 1830. [NRS.AD14.30.86]

MCINTYRE, JOHN, a cottager in Easter Aberfeldy, a petition, 1822. [NRS.GD112.11.118.15.15]

MCINTYRE, MALCOLM, born 1779, a labourer from Callander, emigrated via Port Glasgow aboard the Favourite of St John bound for St John, New Brunswick, on 22 October 1815. [PANB.ms.RS23E.fo.9798]

MCINTYRE, MALCOLM, born 1791 in Balquhidder, of Simpson, McIntyre and Company, died in Montreal, Quebec, on 21 June 1832. [GA.4258]

MCINTYRE, PETER, born 1782, a labourer from Callendar, with his wife Isabella born 1782, and children Jean born 1809, John born 1811, and Janet born 1813, emigrated via Port Glasgow aboard the Favourite of St John bound for St John, New Brunswick, on 22 October 1815. [PANB.ms.RS23E.fo.9798]

MCINTYRE, PETER, born 1791 in Perthshire, a hotelkeeper who was naturalised in South Carolina on 18 July 1839. [NARA.M1183.1]

MCINTYRE, PETER, born 1815, son of Donald McIntyre and his wife Margaret Ferguson, died 1854 in Canada. [Comrie gravestone]

MACINTYRE, THOMAS, born 29 January 1834 in Kilmonivaig, son of Reverend John MacIntyre and his wife Eliza Clark, died in Glenoe, New South Wales, Australia, on 1 October 1911. [F.4.137]

MACINTYRE, WILLIAM, born in Kilmonivaig, son of Duncan MacIntyre a farmer, was educated at Glasgow University in 1829, a minister in New South Wales from 1837 until his death on 12 June 1870. [F.4.594]

MCISAAC, ANN CAMPBELL, youngest daughter of Reverend Patrick McIsaac in Comrie, married John Robertson of Middleton, in Perrysburg, Ohio, on 31 December 1846. [EEC.21463]

MCISAAC, EUPHEMIA, eldest daughter of Reverend Patrick McIsaac in Comrie, married Dr James Robertson, eldest son of Colonel Robertson of Middleton, in Hull Prairie, Ohio, on 13 March 1844. [EEC.20020][W.5.453]

MCKAY, or MCDONALD, born 1789, in 143 South Street, Perth, was accused of uttering forged and base coin in Doune in 1832. [NRS.AD14.32.139]

MCKAY, DUNCAN, with his wife Janet and one child, from Killin, emigrated via Greenock aboard the Curlew bound for Quebec on 21 July 1818. [TNA.CO384/3.123-127]

MCKAY, JAMES, a physician and surgeon in St Thomas in the East, Jamaica, uncle of James McKay a surgeon in Blairgowrie his executor, testament, 1804, Comm. Edinburgh. [NRS]

MCKAY, JAMES, a surgeon in Blairgowrie, father of John McKay in Cairna, papers, 1799-1817. [NRS.GD16.41.999]

MCKAY, JAMES, born 1813, a drover, guilty of cattle theft, was sentenced to transportation, at Perth on 19 April 1833. [PKA.B59.26.11]

MCKAY, JOHN, guilty of housebreaking and theft, was sentenced to transportation to the colonies for seven years, at Perth in September 1834. [PKA.B59.26.11.3.6]

MCKEE, CHRISTINA, born in Cornwall, Glengarry County, Upper Canada, on 25 April 1819, wife of Peter Ireland, died in Perth on 14 November 1849. [Perth, Greyfriars, gravestone]

MCKENNA, HUGH, was accused of murder in Upper Lanrick farm, Kilmadock, in 1846, found guilty and sentenced to twelve months in Perth Tolbooth. [NRS.JC26.1846.33]

MCKENZIE, Mrs ELIZABETH, born 1750, widow of Daniel McKenzie of Glenshee, and mother of William Lyon McKenzie, died in Rochester, New York, on 22 December 1839. [Morning Commercial News, 15.1.1840]

MCKENZIE, JOHN, born 1812, a labourer, son of William McKenzie in Dunblane, was accused of child murder in Ardoch or Braco. [NRS.AD14.35.85]

MACKENZIE, PETER, born 24 March 1809 in Perth, a horticulturalist who emigrated to Philadelphia, Pennsylvania, in 1827, died there on 25 March 1868. [Mount Vernon cemetery, Philadelphia][AP]

MCKENZIE, THOMAS, with Mary Burry his wife, from Dunkeld, emigrated via Greenock on 5 June 1829 aboard the *Albion* bound for Quebec, landed there on 20 Jul 1829, settled in Quebec City and later in Megantic County. [AMC.22]

MCKENZIE, WILLIAM, born 1771 in Perthshire, a farmer in Georgetown, South Carolina, was naturalised on 27 May 1807. [NARA.M1183.1]

MCKENZIE, WILLIAM, born 1804, a mason in Blairgowrie, was accused of assault in 1826. [NRS.AD14.26.159]

MCKARCHAR, JOHN, a leather merchant in Perth, died 4 August 1863, brother of Duncan McKarchar a farmer in Canada West. [NRS.S/H]

MCKERCHAR, ALEXANDER, son of Duncan McKerchar, [1775-1825], and his wife Mary Stewart, [1787-1870], settled in Washington, D.C. [Fortingall gravestone]

MCKERCHAR, DONALD, probably from Perthshire, settled in Reach, Canada West, by 1848. [NRS.GD112.61.5/2]

MCKERCHAR, DONALD, born 1856, son of Donald McKerchar and his wife Isabella McGregor, died in Minneapolis on 4 February 1917. [Fortingall, Kerrowmore, gravestone]

MCKERCHAR, DUNCAN, in Craigie of Balquhidder, a letter, 1801. [NRS.GD112.11.8.2.1]

MCKERCHAR, DUNCAN, probably from Perthshire, settled in Reach, Canada West, by 1848. [NRS.GD112.61.5/2]

MCKERCHAR, JOHN, shepherd of David Sinclair in Little Findowie, Dunkeld, victim of assault, stabbing and wounding in 1828. [NRS.AD14.28.256]

MCKERCHAR, JOHN, probably from Perthshire, settled in Reach, Canada West, by 1848. [NRS.GD112.61.5/2]

MCKERCHAR, WILLIAM, son of Duncan McKerchar, [1775-1825], and his wife Mary Stewart, [1787-1870], settled in Wroxeter, Canada, [Fortingall gravestone]

MACKIE, DAVID, a coppersmith in Perth, 1815. [NRS.GD1.427.16/13]

MCKILLICAN, WILLIAM, born 1776, a minister, formerly of the Congregational Church in Callander, died in Lochiel, Glengarry County, Upper Canada, in November 1849. [W.X.1067] [SG.18.1883]

MCKINLAY, DONALD, born 1779, a labourer from Callendar, with his wife Margaret born 1782, and children Margaret born 1811, and John born 1813, emigrated via Port Glasgow aboard the Favourite of St John bound for St John, New Brunswick, on 22 October 1815. [PANB.ms.RS23E.fo.9798]

MCKINLAY, WILLIAM, Keeper of Dunblane Cathedral in 1849. [NRS.GD1.392.215]

MCLACHLIN, CATHERINE, born 1803 in Perthshire, died in Canada on 11 June 1881. [White Lake gravestone, Renfrew, Ontario]

MCLACHLIN, DUNCAN, born 1803 in Perthshire, died in Canada on 1 October 1881. [White Lake gravestone, Renfrew, Ontario]

MCLACHLAN, WILLIAM, son of William McLachlan, a seaman in Dundee, and his wife Isabel Elder, [1792-1857], settled in Melbourne, Victoria, Australia. [Longforgan gravestone]

MCLAGAN, ALEXANDER, in Borlick of Aberfeldy, a petition in 1826. [NRS.GD112.11.9.2.11]

MCLAGGAN, HENRY, born 1776, a carpenter, lately in Demerara, died in Stix, Perthshire, on 14 February 1827. [Kenmore gravestone]

MCLAGGAN, JOHN, son of Alexander McLaggan a merchant in Auchtergaven, a student at Marischal College, Aberdeen, in 1830s. [MCA]

MCLAGGAN, PETER, a former soldier of the 28$^{th}$ Regiment of Foot, residing in Aberfeldy, versus Elizabeth Malcolm, daughter of David Malcolm a shoemaker in Canongate, Edinburgh, a process of divorce in 1822. [NRS.CC8.6.1847]

MCLAREN, ALEXANDER, born 1773, son of James McLaren, died 17 January 1808, and was buried in Jamaica. [Moulin gravestone]

MCLAREN, ALEXANDER, born 1788, a labourer from Lochearnhead, Balquhidder, with his wife Margaret born 1793, emigrated via Port Glasgow aboard the Favourite of St John bound for St John, New Brunswick, on 22 October 1815. [PANB.ms.RS23E.fo.9798]

MCLAREN, ALEXANDER, in Hunthall, Glendevon, a victim of assault in 1822. [NRS.AD14.22.58]

MCLAREN, ALEXANDER, with his wife and four children, from Blackhills, Perthshire, emigrated via Liverpool to North America in 1833. [SG.II.152]

MCLAREN, ARCHIBALD, born 1796, a labourer from Callendar, emigrated via Port Glasgow aboard the Favourite of St John bound for St John, New Brunswick, on 22 October 1815. [PANB.ms.RS23E.fo.9798]

MCLAREN, CHRISTINE, with two children, from Comrie, emigrated via Greenock aboard the Curlew bound for Quebec on 21 July 1818. [TNA.CO384/3.123-127]

MCLAREN, COLIN, with his wife Christine and two children, from Comrie, emigrated via Greenock aboard the Curlew bound for Quebec on 21 July 1818. [TNA.CO384/3.123-127]

MCLAREN, DONALD, with his wife Marjory, and six children, from Balquhidder, emigrated via Greenock aboard the Sophia of Ayr bound for Quebec on 26 July 1818. [TNA.CO384/3.133-134]

MCLAREN, DONALD, in Shuttlefield Close, South Street, Perth, a victim of theft in 1830. [NRS.AD14.30.21]

MCLAREN, DUNCAN, son of Donald McLaren and his wife Margaret McGregor, settled in New York in 1783, died there on 17 August 1825, buried in Greenwood Cemetery. [Comrie gravestone]

MCLAREN, DUNCAN, a tenant in Wester Struan, Glen Quaich, was fined for having smuggled whisky in 1822. [NRS.GD112.11.8.14.24]

MCLAREN, DUNCAN, born 1773, died in Glengarry, North America, in 1847. [Monzie gravestone]

MCLAREN, DUNCAN, [1813-1895], husband of Margaret Campbell, [1844-1910], parents of Alexander McLaren, born 1882, died in Kansas City, USA, on 16 April 1912. [Dunning gravestone]

MCLAREN, ELIZABETH, widow of John McLaren in Dunning, was the victim of murder, theft and reset in 1823. [NRS.AD14.2311; 2450]

MCLAREN, HELEN, born 1797, died in Glengarry, North America, on 7 March 1868. [Monzie gravestone]

MCLAREN, JANET, born 1791, from Callendar, emigrated via Port Glasgow aboard the Favourite of St John bound for St John, New Brunswick, on 22 October 1815. [PANB.ms.RS23E.fo.9798]

MCLAREN, JOHN, with his wife Catherine and two children, from Comrie, emigrated via Greenock aboard the Curlew bound for Quebec on 21 July 1818. [TNA.CO384/3.123-127]

MCLAREN, JOHN, with his wife Janet and one child, from Killin, emigrated via Greenock aboard the Curlew bound for Quebec on 21 July 1818. [TNA.CO384/3.123-127]

MCLAREN, ROBERT, born 1778, a labourer from Callendar, emigrated via Port Glasgow aboard the Favourite of St John bound for St John, New Brunswick, on 22 October 1815. [PANB.ms.RS23E.fo.9798]

MCLAUGHLIN, STEWART, born 1802, son of John McLaughlin, [1758-1824], a mason in Perth, and his wife Margaret Kidd, [1771-1842], died in New York on 18 June 1855. [Perth, Greyfriars, gravestone]

MCLAUREN, DONALD, born 1770, a farmer from Perthshire, with his wife Eliza born 1771, son James born 1797, daughter Janet born 1799, and son John born 1801, emigrated via Port Glasgow aboard the <u>Commerce</u> bound for Pictou, Nova Scotia, on 10 August 1803. [NLS.ms1053.104-109]

MCLAURIN, EWAN, late Captain of the Breadalbane Fencibles, son of Lieutenant Colonel McLaurin of the South Carolina Loyalists, died in Demerara on 5 May 1810. [EA]; his widow died in Demerara on 29 December 1822. [SM.91.519]

MCLAUREN, WILLIAM, born 1778, a farmer from Perthshire, with his wife Janet born 1783, and son William born 1802, emigrated via Port Glasgow aboard the <u>Commerce</u> bound for Pictou, Nova Scotia, on 10 August 1803. [NLS.ms1053.104-109]

MCLEAN, ALEXANDER, schoolmaster in Aberfeldy, a petition, 1804. [NRS.GD112.11.7.7.14]

MCLEAN, CHARLES, born 1786, a labourer from Fortingall, with his wife Mary born 1787, and daughter Christian born 1807, also his sister Jane McLean born 1788, emigrated aboard the <u>Clarendon of Hull</u> bound for Prince Edward Island, Canada, in August 1808. [NSARM] [TNA.CO226.23]

MCLEAN, CHARLES, an Excise officer in Killin, was accused of assault in 1831. [NRS.AD1431,47]

MCLEAN, CHRISTIAN, wife of John Young a travelling merchant, a prisoner in Perth, was accused of theft, case dismissed on 9 September 1799. [NRS.JC11.44]

MCLEAN, DONALD, born 1790, a labourer from Fortingall, emigrated aboard the <u>Clarendon of Hull</u> bound for Prince Edward Island, Canada, in August 1808. [NSARM][ [TNA.CO226.23]

MCLEAN, JAMES, with his wife Janet and one child, from Killin, emigrated via Greenock aboard the <u>Curlew</u> bound for Quebec Reverend D B. Blair on 21 July 1818. [TNA.CO384/3.123-127]

MCLEAN, JAMES, born 1801 in Perthshire, a resident of Charleston, South Carolina, was naturalised on 6 October 1824. [NARA.M1183.1]

MCLEAN, JOHN, in Corriemuckloch, Crieff, accused of bigamy in 1836. [NRS.AD14.36.81]

MCLEAN, JOHN, a Scottish Society for the Promotion of Christian Knowledge schoolteacher in Wester Aberfeldy, applied for a new schoolhouse there in 1837. [NRS.GD112.11.10.5.2]

MACLEAN, MARY SIBELLA, youngest daughter of Captain H. H. MacLean, married Reverend D. B. Blair, of the Free Church at Barney's River, Pictou, Nova Scotia, on 28 August 1851. [W.XII.1252]

MCLEAN, WILLIAM, and his son John McLean in Carle, Kenmore, with a cartload of smuggled spirits, resisted arrest and assaulted Excisemen in 1808. [NRS.JC26.1808.7]

MCLEISH, JOHN, schoolmaster of Burrelton and Woodside, a petition, 1845. [NRS.GD1.2.51.178]

MCLEISH, ROBERT, born in Perth on 25 December 1832, a headmaster, died on 11 January 1862 in South Africa.

MCLEISH, Reverend WILLIAM, minister of Collace, versus Jean McDuff or McLeish in 1807. [NRS.CS271.63866]

MCLEOD, JAMES, a farm servant in Invermay, Forteviot, was accused of assault in 1837. [NRS.AD37.92]

MCMARTIN, DUNCAN in Aberfeldy, a victim of forgery in 1835. [NRS.AD14.35.80]

MCMILLAN, ALEXANDER, in Aberfeldy, a victim of forgery in 1835. [NRS.AD14.35.80]

MCMILLAN, GEORGE, in Perth Tolbooth in 1827, was accused of theft with violence. [NRS.JC26.1827.392]

MCMILLAN, JAMES, born 1752 in Perthshire, died at the residence of John King in Studholm, King's County, New Brunswick, on 14 December 1843. [New Brunswick Courier.13.1.1844]

MACNAB, ALEXANDER, born 1762 in Glen Dochart, Killin, settled in Nova Scotia, died on 11 May 1824. [MacNab's Hill gravestone, South Shore, Malagash, Cumberland County, NS]

MACNAB, ALEXANDER, of Innishewan, Perthshire, a letter, 1793. [NLS.Acc.6945]

MCNAB, CHARLOTTE, in Kincanathie, Scone, a victim of theft in 1837. [NRS.AD14.37.163]

MCNAB, DUNCAN, with his wife Catherine, and three children, from Killin, emigrated via Greenock aboard the Curlew bound for Quebec on 21 July 1818. [TNA.CO384/3.123-127]

MCNAB, DUNCAN, guilty of forgery, was sentenced to transportation to the colonies for seven years, at Perth in April 1832. [PKA.B59.26.11.3.6]

MCNAB, DUNCAN, born 30 December 1820 in New York, son of John McNab, died in New Scone on 27 March 1854. [Muthill, Innerpeffrey gravestone]

MCNAB, FRANCIS, of McNab, of Kinnell, Killin, a letter 1806. [NRS.GD13.121]

MCNAB, JAMES, born 1817, son of John McNab, [1757-1837], and his wife Christine Buchanan, [1786-1845], died in Arthur township, Canada, on 29 March 1872. [Callander gravestone]

MCNAB, JOHN, born 1782, 'formerly in New York', died in New Scone on 12 March 1858. [Muthill Innerpeffrey gravestone] [NRS.S/H]

MCNAB, JOHN, a mason in Callendar, was accused of assault in 1831. [NRS.AD14.31.47]

MCNAB, MARY, in Kincanathie, Scone, a victim of theft in 1837. [NRS.AD14.37.163]

MCNAB, PETER, a stocking weaver in Killin, a letter 1806. [NRS.GD112.11.7.9.44]

MCNAB, PETER, postmaster in Killin, a letter in 1807. [NRS.GD112.11.8.1.23]

MCNAB, ROBERT, a mason in Killin, applied for the property there previously occupied by Dr Campbell, 1807. [NRS.GD112.11.8.1.38]

MCNAB, ......, sons of Alexander McNab of Inishewan, emigrated to America in 1793. [NLS.Acc.6945]

MCNAUGHTON, ALEXANDER, with his wife Elizabeth, from Dull, emigrated via Greenock aboard the Curlew bound for Quebec on 21 July 1818. [TNA.CO384/3.123-127]

MCNAUGHTON, CHRISTINE, born 1818, daughter of John McNaughton, a farmer, [1779-1853], and his wife Isabella Stewart, [1784-1857], wife of Reverend Duncan Cameron, died in Lucknow, Canada, on 16 August 1885. [Logerait gravestone]

MCNAUGHTON, DONALD, in Wester Castran, Balquhidder, accused of assault in 1825. [NRS.JC26.1825.295]

MCNAUGHTON, JOHN, of the Aberfeldy Inn, a letter, 1807. [NRS.GD112.11.8.2.24]

MCNAUGHTON, JOHN, late wright in Aberfeldy, now in Leith, versus the Earl of Breadalbane, 1828. [NRS.GD112.11.9.4.34]

MCNAUGHTON, MALCOLM, born 1782, from Strathfillan, emigrated via Port Glasgow aboard the Favourite of St John bound for St John, New Brunswick, on 22 October 1815. [PANB.ms.RS23E.fo.9798]

MCNAUGHTON, PATRICK, in Inch, Little Dunkeld, a victim of horse theft in 1831. [NRS.AD1431.14]

MCNAUGHTON, PETER, in Monzie, a sequestration petition, 1840. [NRS.CS279.1690]

MCNAUGHTON, WILLIAM, born 1780, a labourer from Fortingall, with his wife Margaret born 1781, emigrated aboard the Clarendon of Hull bound for Prince Edward Island, Canada, in August 1808. [NSARM] [TNA.CO226.23]

MCNICOL, DONALD, in Lotts, Callendar, found guilty of assault and sentenced to six months imprisonment in 1819. [NRS.JC11.60]

MCNIVEN, ALEXANDER, in Bowerswell Road, Perth, dead by 1848, uncle of William McNiven in Schenectady College, New York. [NRS.S/H]

MCOWAN, PETER, from Comrie, later in Canada, dead by 1849, brother of Mary McOwan or Bayne in Muthil. [NRS.S/H]

MCPHEE, ANGUS, from Crieff, with his wife and three children, emigrated via Fort William aboard the Jean of Irvine bound for Quebec in June 1802. [PAC.mg24.1183]

MACPHERSON, ALLAN, son of Allan MacPherson and his wife Elizabeth in Blairgowrie, emigrated to Berbice in 1804, a planter, soldier, and chaplain in the West Indies, later in India. [NRS.NRAS.0057.bundle 8/10]

MCPHERSON, Colonel ALLAN, of Blairgowrie, letters, 1781-1808. [NRS.GD80.907]

MCPHERSON, CHARLES, born 1753 in Perthshire, a grocer, emigrated via England to New York in 1776, a Loyalist who settled in New Brunswick in 1783, husband of Catherine McLeod, died in St John, N.B., on 6 July 1823. [City Gazette, 10.7.1823]

MCPHERSON, JAMES, born 1783, late from Essequibo, died in Perth on 13 March 1848. [Perth, Greyfriars, gravestone]

MCPHERSON, MARGARET, born 1824, daughter of Angus McPherson in Keith Bank, Rattray, accused of theft in 1841. [NRS.AD14.41.210]

MCPHERSON, MARY, daughter of Jean McGregor or McPherson a widow in Pitcairngreen, Redgorton, 1835. [NRS.AD14.35.86]

MCPHERSON, WILLIAM, a hostler in the service of Thomas Marshall a vintner in Perth, testament, 1792, Comm. St Andrews. [NRS]

MCPHERSON, WILLIAM, son of Allan McPherson and his wife Elizabeth in Blairgowrie, was a planter in Berbice around 1806. [NRS.NRAS.bundle 8/10]

MCPHERSON, JAMES, born 1795, a labourer from Dalverack, Monyvair, emigrated via Greenock aboard the William of New York bound for New York, landed there on 17 October 1817. [NY Municipal Archives] [NY Commercial Advertiser, 18.10.1817]

MCQUEEN, JAMES, born 1798, a blacksmith from Kilmadock, emigrated to Upper Canada in 1822, settled in Esquesing in 1824, and in Pilkington in 1846. [Wellington County Museum, ms.45a.981.85]

MCREICH, JOHN, in Killin, applied for a pendicle there in 1807. [NRS.GD112.11.8.2.22]

MCRITCHIE, GEORGE, in New Scone in 1848. [NRS.CS313.575]

MCRITCHIE, JEAN, servant in Little Findowie, Dunkeld, was accused of assaulting, stabbing, and wounding, in 1828. [NRS.AD14.28.256]

MCTAVISH, or CAMPBELL, ALEXANDER, late tenant in the Braes of Moness, now in Aberfeldy, parish of Dull, a petition in 1807. [NRS.GD112.11.8.3.13]

MCTAVISH, ALEXANDER, with his wife Catherine and two children, from Dull, emigrated via Greenock aboard the Curlew bound for Quebec on 21 July 1818. [TNA.CO384/3.123-127]

MCTAVISH, JOHN, from Dull, emigrated via Greenock aboard the Curlew bound for Quebec on 21 July 1818. [TNA.CO384/3.123-127]

MCTAVISH, JOHN, with his wife Margaret and two children, from Dull, emigrated via Greenock aboard the Curlew bound for Quebec on 21 July 1818. [TNA.CO384/3.123-127]

MCTAVISH, JOHN, with his wife Catherine, from Dull, emigrated via Greenock aboard the Curlew bound for Quebec on 21 July 1818. [TNA.CO384/3.123-127]

MCVEAN, ARCHIBALD, son of Reverend Patrick McVean in Kenmore, died in Grenada on 7 September 1822. [DPCA.1066]

MCVEAN, JAMES, tacksman of Inshdaive, Breadalbane, to emigrate to Nova Scotia in 1785. [NRS.GD112.16.4.1.2]

MCVEAN, Mrs MARY, from Killin, emigrated via Greenock aboard the Curlew bound for Quebec on 21 July 1818. [TNA.CO384/3.123-127]

MCVIE, JOHN, with his wife Janet and five children, from Balquhidder, emigrated via Greenock aboard the Sophia of Ayr bound for Quebec on 26 July 1818. [TNA.CO384/3.133-134]

MCVIE, JOHN, with his wife Janet and two children from Comrie, emigrated via Greenock aboard the Curlew bound for Quebec on 21 July 1818. [TNA.CO384/3.123-127]

MAILER, JOHN, son of John Mailer a brewer in Auchterarder, was apprenticed to Alexander Hay and Neil Ferguson saddlers and harness makers in Perth for four years, 1812. [NRS.GD1.427/16/11]

MAILER, JOHN, born 1815, a slater in Auchterarder, accused of poaching in 1835. [NRS.AD14.35.100]

MAILER, WILLIAM, in Middlethird, Pitcairn, Dunning, accused of murder in 1824. [NRS.AD14.24.66]

MALCOLM, JOHN, son of Jean Malcolm in Madderty, settled in Norfolk, Virginia, probate, December 1793, PCC. [TNA]

MALLOCH, ANDREW, a writer in Dunblane, died 4 February 1838, father of James Christal Malloch in Chisholm Square, New York. [NRS.S/H.1872]; Letters prior to 1828. [NRS.CC6.15.6]

MALLOCH, CATHERINE, a widow in Mill Row, Dunblane, was victim of hamesucken and an assault in 1830. [NRS.AD14.31.20]

MALLOCH, JAMES, born 1835, son of James Malloch and his wife Janet Shorthouse, died in Spencerport, America, on 18 March 1860. [Forgandenny gravestone]

MALTMAN, JOHN, a mason and wright in Auchterarder, dead by 1824, father of James Maltman a stonecutter from Perth then in New York. [NRS.S/H]

MANN, JOHN, born 1797, a labourer from Kenmore, emigrated via Port Glasgow aboard the <u>Favourite of St John</u> bound for St John, New Brunswick, on 22 October 1815. [PANB.ms.RS23E.fo.9798] [author of 'Travels in North America', Glasgow, 1824]

MANSON, DAVID, born 1783, son of John Manson, a merchant in Perth, and his wife Elizabeth Keay, died in Jamaica on 2 July 1821. [Perth, Greyfriars, gravestone]

MARSHALL, MARGARET, servant to William Graham tenant in Teuchathill, Madderty, was accused of concealment of pregnancy and child murder in 1820. [NRS.AD14.20.142]

MARSHALL, THOMAS HAY, commandant of the $2^{nd}$ Battalion of the Royal Perth Volunteers, a bond, 1807. [PKA.B59.24.6.137]

MARTIN, MARGARET, sister of David Martin a labourer in Alan Street, Blairgowrie, was accused of concealing a pregnancy in 1821. [NRS.AD14.21.14]

MARTIN, Dr PETER, a physician in Dunning, and factor of Lord Rollo of Duncrub, an account book, 1822-1829. [NRS.GD56.163.4]

MARTIN, Captain, master of the Fair City of Perth bound from Perth to Australia, landed at Melbourne, Victoria, Australia, on 6 December 1854. [LCL.4786]

MASON, GILBERT, failed to appear for jury service in 1811. [NRS.JC26.1811.25]

MASON, ROBERT, an auctioneer in Perth, who uttered counterfeit coins, was outlawed in 1799. [NRS.JC11]

MATTHEW, AMELIA, born 1774, wife of James Cameron formerly a merchant and banker in Dunkeld, died in New York on 23 January 1840. [EEC.20040]

MATHEWSON, JOHN, a feuar in Stanley, dead by 1843, father of Donald Mathewson in Johnstown, USA. [NRS.S/H]

MAXTON, Reverend ALEXANDER, minister at Fowlis Wester, in Redford, Madderty, in 1829. [NRS.GD155.312]

MAXTON, ANTHONY, of Cultaquhey, a letter to Robert Moncrieff in 1819. [NRS.GD155.924]

MAXTON, JOHN, born 1787 in Crieff, a baker in Charleston, South Carolina, was naturalised on 4 February 1825. [NARA.M1183.1]

MAXWELL, PATRICK JOSEPH, a trader and tenant farmer in Killin, 1846. [NRS.CS280.8.15]

MEIK, JOHN, youngest son of Reverend Patrick Meik minister of Kinnoull, died in St Vincent in January 1794. [EA.3160.230]

MELDRUM, DAVID, of Dron, versus Mrs Catherine Hendry or Meldrum, a decreet 1814. [NRS.CS38.10.36]; also, versus Robert Meldrum of Bonnytown, a decreet, 1817. [NRS.CS40.25.58]

MELDRUM, THOMAS, son of Robert Meldrum and his wife Elizabeth Rankine, [1794-1885], settled in Vindex, Multaburra, Queensland, Australia. [Abernethy gravestone]

MELLISH, JOHN, born 1771 in Perthshire, emigrated to America in 1809, a geographer who died in Philadelphia, Pennsylvania, on 30 December 1822. [Georgia Republican.13.1.1823]

MELLIS, WILLIAM, from Perthshire, a merchant in Savanna, Georgia, died in Darien, Georgia, on 7 August 1811. [Colonial Museum and Savanna Advertiser, 5.9.1811]

MELVILLE, GEORGE, in Leonard Street, Perth, was accused of housebreaking and theft in 1825. [NRS.JC26.295]

MELVILLE, JOHN, born 1846, son of Charles Melville and his wife Mary Duffus, died in Addington Hospital, Durban, South Africa, on 24 May 1901. [Rattray gravestone]

MENZIES, ARCHIBALD, in Kingston, Jamaica, appointed Colin Menzies in the Mains of Ballechan, Logerait, as factor re the estate of Pitnacree, Logerait, in 1809. [NRS.RD3.333.921]

MENZIES, ARCHIBALD, born 1808, a baker and grocer in Aberfeldy, accused of forgery in 1835. [NRS.AD14.35.80]; sequestration in 1835. [NRS.CS232.M56.11/M53.7]

MENZIES, Mrs CATHERINE, wife of Robert Menzies in Kirkton of Weem, was accused of theft and reset, however, as she did not understand English the case was dismissed on 10 May 1800. [NRS.JC11.44]

MENZIES, CHARLES, born 1823, son of Alexander Menzies and his wife Ann Fisher, died in Victoria, Australia, on 9 March 1866. [Moneydie, Logiealmond, gravestone]

MENZIES, DUNCAN, from Aberfeldy, married Maggie Whittet, daughter of Alexander Whittet a blacksmith in Auchtermuchty, Fife, in St Joseph, USA, on 10 October 1873. [FH]

MENZIES, JAMES, jr., a militia rioter at Castle Menzies, was sentenced to transportation to the colonies for seven years, at Perth on 7 May 1798. [AJ.2627]

MENZIES, JAMES, a shoemaker in Comrie, died 14 February 1849, father of Thomas Menzies a merchant in Peterboro, Canada. [NRS.S/H.1877]

MENZIES, JOHN, son of Daniel Menzies a merchant in Weem, was apprenticed to Parlane McFarlane a blacksmith and farrier in Perth, for three years in 1804. [NRS.GD1.427.16/7]

MENZIES, JOHN, son of Alexander Menzies and his wife Ann Fisher, died in Victoria, Australia, on 14 April 1878. [Moneydie, Logiealmond, gravestone]

MENZIES, JOHN, born 1856, son of William Menzies and his wife Christina McPherson, died 27 December 1892 in Queensland, Australia. [Dull gravestone]

MENZIES, PETER, born 1822, son of Alexander Menzies and his wife Ann Fisher, died in Victoria in 1852. [Moneydie, Logiealmond, gravestone]

MENZIES, ROBERT, in Hillyland, Tibbermuir, was a victim of embezzlement in 1849. [NRS.AD14.49.93]

MENZIES, RUTHVEN, born 1820, son of Archibald Menzies, died in Melbourne, Australia, in March 1883. [Perth, Greyfriars, gravestone]

MENZIES, THOMAS, son of James Menzies, died 1849, and his wife Isabella MacIntyre, [died 1841], settled in Peterborough, Canada. [Comrie gravestone]

MENZIES, WILLIAM, son of John Menzies, [1788-1867], a farmer in Lurcan, and his wife Christianna Munro, [1787-1863], settled in Wisconsin. [Weem gravestone]

MENZIES, WILLIAM, a farmer in Kirkhill, Trinity Gask, accused of poaching in 1825. [NRS.JC26.1825.295]

MENZIES, WIILIAM, and his wife Christina McPherson, were parents of John Menzies, born 1856, died in Queensland, Australia, on 27 December 1892. [Dull gravestone]

MICHIE, DAVID KINLOCH, was accused of assault with a loaded firearm at Balnabrioch Hill, Glendelvine, in 1845. [NRS.AD14.45.291]

MIDDLEMISS, HELEN, in Kincanathie, Scone, a victim of theft in 1837. [NRS.AD14.37.163]

MILL, JAMES, and THOMAS, farmers at Bridgeton of Islabank, sederunt book, 1802-1803. [NRS.CS96.7061]

MILL, JAMES, a weaver in New Scone, accused of exposing a child to the danger of its life in 1820, sentenced to four months in Perth Tolbooth in 1820. [NRS.AC14.20.141; JC26.1820.115]

MILL, JAMES, born 1817, a farm servant at Baigley, Dron, accused of poaching in 1836. [NRS.AD14.36.457]

MILL, PETER, born 1817, miller at Dron Mill, accused of poaching in 1836. [NRS.AD14.36.457]

MILLER, DAVID, a house carpenter in Auchterarder, a contract, 1839. [NRS.GD152.218.6.14]

MILLER, DAVID, born 1841, son of James Miller and his wife Isabel Young, died 31 March 1888 in Dunedin, New Zealand. [Methven gravestone]

MILLER, GEORGE, carter in Muthill, accused of assault in Glendevon in 1822. [NRS.AD14.22.58]

MILLER, GEORGE, in Murrayshall, died in 1834, father of Isabella Miller and Mary Ann Miller or Hunt, also William Miller in Mordstone, Canada West. [NRS.S/H.1851]

MILLER, JAMES, a mason in Crieff, accounts, 1806-1810. [NRS.GD241.682]

MILLER, JAMES, a writer in Coupar Angus, versus Francis Keill in Monorgan, a decreet, 1815. [NRS.CS42.13.56]

MILLER, JAMES, jr., in Coupar Angus, agent for the Perth Union Bank, versus Thomas Wallace in 1818. [NRS.CS271.68839]; agent for Peter Robertson in Jamaica, a letter in 1822. [NRS.GD132.159]

MILLER, JOHN, from Cluny, a member of the Scots Charitable Society of Boston, New England, in 1817. [SCS/NEHGS]

MILLER, JOHN, born 1803, in Kinpauch, Blackford, was accused of sending a threatening letter in 1833. [NRS.AD14.33.416]

MILLER, or RINTOUL, MARY, wife of James Rintoul in Little Seggie, Orwell, a housebreaker in 1837, was sentenced to twelve months in Kinross Tolbooth. [NRS.AD14.37.205; JC26.1837.290]

MILLER, ROBERT, sr., in Milnathort, Kinross, a victim of rioting in Dollar, Clackmannan, in 1837. [NRS.AD14.37.475]

MILLAR, WALTER, son of Walter Millar in Perth, a student at Marischal College, Aberdeen, in 1830. [MCA]

MILLER, WILLIAM, doorkeeper at Deanstoun Cotton Works, Kilmadock, was accused of theft in 1832. [NRS.AD14.32.16]

MILNE, GEORGE, in Errol, a prisoner in Perth, was accused of housebreaking and wheel theft in 1820. [NRS.JC26.1820.10]

MILNE, JOHN, son of James Milne of Milnefield, a student in Marischal College around 1800. [MCA]

MILN, or MILLS, JOHN, a wheelwright in Perth, died 31 January 1861, father of Peter Drummond Mills in Ponce, Puerto Rico. [NRS.S/H.1863]

MITCHELL, ANDREW, from Perthshire, a shopkeeper in Charleston, South Carolina, probate, 11 June 1796, S.C.

MITCHELL, DAVID BRYDIE, born 22 October 1766, son of John Mitchell in Muthill, settled in Savanna, Georgia, Governor of Georgia, died in Milledgeville, Georgia, on 22 April 1837. [WA]

MITCHELL, JAMES, at the toll bar of Scone, 1813. [PKA.B59.35.64]

MITCHELL, JAMES, son of John Mitchell a shoemaker in Perth, a student at Marischal College in 1812. [MCA]

MITCHELL, JOHN, born 1822, son of Hugh Mitchell and his wife Margaret Small, died in Sydney, Australia, on 4 July 1863. [New Scone gravestone]

MITCHELL, JOHN, jr., in Blairgowrie, a sequestration petition, 1842. [NRS.CS279.1421]

MITCHELL, JOHN, son of Thomas Mitchell a tax-collector in Blair Atholl, was educated at Marischal College in Aberdeen in 1846. [MCA]

MITCHELL, ROBERT, born 1 July 1776 in Perth, a merchant in Savanna, Georgia, died on 26 December 1830. [Old Colonial Cemetery, Savanna, gravestone]

MITCHELL, THOMAS, in Blairgowrie, a victim of forgery in 1824. [NRS.AD14.24.101]

MITCHELL, WILLIAM, born 1760 in Perthshire, a mariner in Charleston, South Carolina, was naturalised on 25 July 1820. [NARA.M1183.1]

MOIR, JOHN, born 1809, a wright, c/o Robert Moir, The Cross, Dunblane, was accused of arson in 1833. [NRS.AD14.33.29]

MONCRIEFF, ARCHIBALD, born 29 June 1751, son of Reverend Sir William Moncrieff and his wife Katherine Wellwood in Blackford, a merchant in Baltimore, Maryland, died 1803. [F.4.262]

MONCREIFF, FRANCIS EDWARD, born 1858, son of George Moncreiff and his wife Angela Birch, died in Toronto, Canada, on 7 January 1884. [Perth, Wellshill, gravestone]

MONCREIFF, JAMES, a brass-founder in Perth in 1812. [NRS.GD1.427.16/]

MONCREIFF, JOHN, born in Perthshire, settled in Charleston, South Carolina, before 1772, a Loyalist in 1776, died 12 May 1821. [Old Scots gravestone, Charleston] [TNA.AO.13.131.452]

MONCUR, GEORGE, a soldier of the Tayside Fencible Regiment, a prisoner in Perth accused of robbery, was found guilty and sentenced to death by hanging on 11 September 1799. [NRS.JC11.44]

MOON, CHRISTIAN, born 1786, from Blair, emigrated aboard the Clarendon of Hull bound for Prince Edward Island, Canada, in August 1808. [NSARM] [TNA.CO226.23]

MOON, GEORGE, born 1781, a labourer from Strathgarry, emigrated aboard the Clarendon of Hull bound for Prince Edward Island, Canada, in August 1808. [NSARM] [TNA.CO226.23]

MOON, HELEN, in Crosscauseway, Perth, a court witness in 1822. [NRS.AD14.22.121]

MOON, JOHN, in Clunes of Glengarry, a bond of caution, in 1800. [NRS.CS27.1.19796]

MORAY, JAMES, of Abercairny, 1830s. [NRS.GD24.1.736]

MORRIS, JAMES, born 1831, son of James Morris and his wife Betsy Gibb, died in Queensland, Australia, in 1882. [Collace gravestone]

MORRIS, MARGARET, eldest daughter of James Morris a preacher in Cargill, and his wife Rebecca, daughter of Laurence Day the tacksman of Cargill, papers, 1801-1806. [NRS.GD160.368]

MORRIS, WILLIAM, in Pitmiddle, Kinnaird, a victim of theft and reset in 1831. [NRS.AD14.31.54]

MORRISON, ALEXANDER, a worker at John Cassel's distillery at Kepp, Dunblane, was accused of hamesucken in 1825. [NRS.AD14.25.248]

MORISON, DAVID, a weaver in Milnathort, Kinross, was accused of assault in 1837. [NRS.AD14.37.164]

MORRISON, HENRY, in Meal Vennel, Perth, a victim of theft in 1832. [NRS.AD14.29.129]

MORRISON, JOHN, a butcher at Crook of Devon, was accused of theft from Ashintool farm in 1832. [NRS.AD14.32.190]

MORRISON, MARGARET GORDON, daughter of Eneas Morrison in Perthshire, married Dr Tremain from Prince Edward Island, Canada, in Halifax, Nova Scotia, on 16 October 1843. [Times, 31.10.1843]

MORRISON, ROBERT, with his wife and son, from Crieff, emigrated via Greenock aboard the Portaferry bound for Quebec in May 1832. [Quebec Mercury, 13.6.1832]

MORISON, ROBERT, a painter in Perth, dead by 1853, father of Robert Morison, a merchant in Havanna, Cuba. [NRS.S/H.]

MORRISON, THOMAS, a brewer in Milnathort, Kinross, eldest son of the late William Morrison in Whithorn, Kinross, a petition, 1829. [NRS.SC12.6.189.12]

MORISON, WILLIAM, born 1748 in Auchlines, a minister in Londonderry, New Hampshire, from 1783, husband of Jean Fullarton, died in September 1829. [Imm.NE.140]

MORRISON, WILLIAM, a brewer in Kinross, a tack of the lands of Hilton of Burleigh, Orwell, Kinross, 1800. [NRS.GD1.675.20]

MORTON, Captain, master of the Atlantic of Perth was shipwrecked off Cape Francois, Canada, on 5 May 1840. [EEC.20062]

MUDIE, or ROBERTSON, CHRISTIAN, in Dunning, dead by 1825, mother of Margaret Mudie in Douglas, Nova Scotia. [NRS.S/H]

MUNN, WILLIAM, born 1785, a labourer from Kenmore, emigrated via Port Glasgow aboard the Favourite of St John bound for St John, New Brunswick, on 22 October 1815. [PANB.ms.RS23E.fo.9798]

MUNROE, DONALD, with his wife Mary, and three children, from Balquhidder, emigrated via Greenock aboard the Sophia of Ayr bound for Quebec on 26 July 1818. [TNA.CO384/3.133-134]

MUNRO, JOHN, jr., in Aberfeldy, petitioned to build a house at the Square there, he was son of John Munro a carrier in Easter Aberfeldy, 1807. [NRS.GD112.11.8.1.3/4]

MURDOCH, DAVID, born 1768 in Perthshire, emigrated to Pictou, Nova Scotia, in 1801, died there on 8 March 1841. [The Nova Scotian, 25.3.1841]

MURIE, JAMES, a weaver in Dunning, was accused of poaching in 1832. [NRS.AD14.32.97]

MURRAY, CHARLES, born 1812, son of Reverend Andrew Murray, [1754-1844], and his wife Janet Mackie, died in Louisiana, in 1853. [Auchterarder gravestone]

MURRAY, HELEN AMELIA ADELAIDE KEITH, second daughter of Sir William Keith Murray of Ochtertyre, died on 28 January 1869 aboard the Dunbar Castle when bound for Sydney, Australia. [AJ.6329]

MURRAY, HENRY, a weaver in Croft, Blairgowrie, was accused of housebreaking in 1827. [NRS.AD14.27.197]

MURRAY, JAMES, a prisoner in Perth Tolbooth, guilty of threatening the Duke of Atholl with death, was sentenced to transportation to the colonies for life in 1820. [NRS.JC26.1820.115]

MURRAY, JOHN, son of John Murray in Balnabrioch farm, Glendelvine, victim of assault in 1845. [NRS.AD14.45.291]

MURRAY, JOHN, of Kinloch, Glen Quaich, dead by 1848. [NRS.S/H]

MURRAY, THOMAS, in Blairgowrie, a sequestration petition, 1840. [NRS.CS279.1610]

MURRAY, THOMAS, born 1833, son of Henry Murray and his wife Janet Petrie, died on Green Island, Otago, New Zealand, on 26 December 1914. [Kirkmichael gravestone]

MYLES, ROBERT, from Perth, died in Antigua on 6 December 1803. [EA.4082.03]

NEILSON, JOSEPH, son of William Neilson, [1803-1898], and his wife Mary Finlayson, [1811-1898], died in America on 5 November 1871. [Dunblane gravestone]

NICHOLSON, JAMES, miller in Aberfeldy, a petition re repairs to the mill, in 18... [NRS.GD112.11.8.9.9]

NICOL, ALEXANDER, son of John Nicol a shoemaker in Dunkeld, was accused of assault in 1821. [NRS.AD14.21.89]

NICOLL, GEORGE, late in Jamaica, was granted the lands of Arthurstone on 3 July 1789. [NRS.RGS.125.158]

NICOLL, JAMES, a merchant in Errol, 1850. [NRS.CS280.36.107]

NICOLL, ROBERT, master of the Providence of Perth from Dundee to New York in May 1819. [NRS.CE70.1.15]

NICOLSON, JAMES, in Aberfeldy, a letter re the lands of Hugh Cameron late miller in Aberfeldy, 1805. [NRS.GD112.11.7.8.21]

NIVEN, ANDREW, from Alyth, a divinity student in 1828, later a minister in Stirling, then in Jamaica, died in 1846. [UPC]

NIVEN, DUNCAN, from Alyth, emigrated via Greenock aboard the Portaferry bound for Quebec in May 1832. [Quebec Mercury, 13.6.1832]

OATS, CHARLES, schoolmaster in Glendevon, 1836. [NRS.CS271.65506]

OLIPHANT, ANDREW, a farm servant in Invermay, Forteviot, was accused of assault in 1837. [NRS.AD37.92]

OLIPHANT, JAMES BLAIR, of Gask, versus Major General George Duncan Robertson of Strowan, 1830. [NRS.CS271.53741]

OLIPHANT, JANET, of Bachilton, sister and heir of Margaret Oliphant or Cumming in Methven, widow of Alexander Mackenzie in Jamaica, 1801. [NRS.S/H]

ORROCK, ROBERT, a merchant in Milnathort, Kinross, in 1837. [NRS.CS230.SEQN.0.1.3]

OSWALD, JAMES, an Exciseman in Doune, Kilmadock, was assaulted by spirit smugglers in 1808. [NRS.JC26.1808.7]

OVENSTONE, JOHN, in Errol, a sequestration petition, 1840. [NRS.CS279.2005]

PALMER, JOHN, son of Thomas Palmer [1792-1872] and his wife Janet Maxwell [1792-1848], died in Brisbane, Australia, on 2 July 1898. [Kinnoull gravestone]

PALMER, THOMAS, son of Thomas Palmer [1792-1872] and his wife Janet Maxwell [1792-1848], died in Brisbane, Australia, on 22 July 1884. [Kinnoull gravestone]

PATERSON, ANDREW, in Milnathort, Kinross, a victim of rioting in Dollar in 1837. [NRS.AD14.37.475]

PATERSON, BARBARA, a widow in Milnathort, Kinross, a victim of theft and fraud in 1846. [NRS.JC26.1847.637]

PATTERSON, Mrs JESSIE, born 1830, wife of James Rossie, died in Topeka, Kansas, on 24 February 1905. [Dunning gravestone]

PATTERSON, JOHN, born 1814, a copperplate printer, guilty of robbery, was sentenced to transportation to the colonies, at Perth on 17 September 1832. [PKA.B59.26.11]

PATON, CHRISTIAN, versus the Kirk Session of Little Dunkeld, 1823. [NRS.CS44.44.21]

PATTON, JAMES, born 1855, son of David Patton and his wife Lillias Rintoul, died in Oxenford, Queensland, on 25 May 1901. [Methven gravestone]

PAUL, HENRY, in Scotlandwell, Kinross, accused of assault and poaching in 1830. [NRS.AD14.30.8]

PAUL, JAMES, born 1832, son of John Paul, a mason in Perth, and his wife Catherine Whytock, died in Buenos Ayres, Argentina, on 12 December 1867. [Greyfriars gravestone, Perth]

PEACOCK, WILLIAM, in Cargill, a grain and cattle dealer in 1844. [NRS.CS280.30.87]

PEARSON, MARGARET, widow of James Pearson a merchant in Dunblane, versus Andrew Gardner in Blainroar, 1814. [NRS.CS32.9.49]

PEDDIE, JAMES, a surgeon in Perth, accounts, 1794-1800. [PKA.B59.24.6.172]

PEDDIE, JOAN, born 1844, daughter of William Peddie and his wife Agnes Imrie, died in La Cros, Wisconsin, on 13 July 1916. [Perth, Greyfriars, gravestone]

PEDDIE, JOHN, son of Alexander Peddie, [1777-1859], died in America aged 20. [Perth, Greyfriars, gravestone]

PEDDIE, PETER, born 1763 in Perthshire, died in St John, New Brunswick, on 1 December 1836. [Weekly Chronicle, 2.12.1836]

PEDDIE, PETER, in Forteviot, was accused of falsehood and forgery in 1819. [NRS.JC26.1819.85]

PEDDIE, ROBERT, born 1776 in Crieff, a merchant who died in Charleston, South Carolina, on 3 August 1801. [CM: 21.8.1801]

PEDDIE, ROBERT, in Perth, a letter, 1813. [PKA.B59.38.5.44]

PEDDIE, ROBERT, a writer in Perth, factor to Robert Alexander Bannerman of Abernyte, 1820-1825. [PKA.B59.38.5.67]

PENTLAND, GEORGE, a coach and harness maker in Perth, 1809. [NRS.GD24.1.682]

PETER, ALEXANDER, a farmer and auctioneer in Gillybank, Moneydie, was accused of discharging firearms in 1842. [NRS.AD14.42.88]

PETER, ROBERT, agent for the Central Bank of Scotland in Aberfeldy, 1849. [NRS.GD1.408.59]

PETRIE, CHARLES, from Kirkmichael, emigrated via Liverpool to North America in June 1833. [SG.2.152]

PETRIE, WILLIAM, in Errol, was accused of illegally fishing in the Tay in 1848. [NRS.GD155.546]

PIPER, FRANCES, a servant of the Earl of Mansfield at Scone, versus James Halthorne a writer in Edinburgh who married in Maybole in 1810, a process of adherence in 1823, [NRS.CC8.6.1884]; and a process of divorce in 1823. [NRS.CC8.6.1900]

PIRNIE, JOHN, born 22 July 1791 in Moss-side, Redgorton, son of James Pirnie and his wife Elizabeth Herries, emigrated via Greenock to America by 1817, naturalised in New York on 3 March 1820, a distiller in New York by 1831, died there on 20 February 1862. [ANY][NY Court of Common Pleas]

PIRNIE, PETER, an accountant from Perthshire, emigrated via Greenock to America, was naturalised in New York on 2 April 1821. [NY Court of Common Pleas]

PIRRIE, JOHN, born 1816, son of John Pirrie, postmaster in Perth, and his wife Jessie Ramsay, a private soldier of the 91$^{st}$ Regiment, died in Grahamstown, South Africa, on 27 September 1847. [Wellshill gravestone, Perth]

PIRIE, J. T., son of Allan Pirie, [1796-1874], a merchant in New York. [Errol gravestone]

PITCAIRN, ROBERT, born 1767, a merchant from Perth, was admitted as a burgess of Klepediai in 1807. [Geschicht der Koniglich Preussischen See und Handelsstadt Memel]

PITCAIRN, ROBERT, of Pitblae, heir to Andrew Pitcairn of Hilton, letters of horning, 1804. [NRS.GD1.675.27]; dead by 15 January 1825. [NRS.GD1.675.91]; correspondence with Robert Pitcairn in Spanish Town, Jamaica, from 1792 to 1823. [NRS.GD1.675.143]

PITCAIRN, WILLIAM, in Milnathort, Kinross, son of the late Robert Pitcairn, a letter 1825. [NRS.GD1.675.124]

PITCAITHLY, MARGARET, born 1827, wife of George Bruce, died in Christchurch, New Zealand, on 26 May 1876. [Kettins gravestone]

PITKAITHLY, ROBERT, petitioned to erect a stone in Perth graveyard in 1804. [PKA.B59.24.510]

PLAYFAIR, JOHN, a wright in Coupar Angus, trustee of James and John Hutchison in 1816. [NRS.CS36.17.54]

PORTEOUS, JOHN, a feuar in Muthill, dead by 1793, father of John Porteous a merchant in New York. [NRS.S/H]

PORTEOUS, JOHN, from Muthill, settled in Herkimer County, New York, 1786, [NRS.CS17.1.5.224]; probate 13 June 1799, N.Y.

PORTEOUS, JOHN, born 1802, son of David Porteous in Crieff, died in India on 24 July 1834. [Scotch Burial Ground, Calcutta]

PORTEOUS, JOHN, a merchant in Perth, failed to appear for jury service in 1811. [NRS.JC26.1811.25]

PRINGLE, JAMES, born 1808, a farmer in Graymond, Bendochy, was accused of theft and destroying a trust disposition in Forfar 1848. [NRS.AC14.48.421]

PRINGLE, JOHN, born 1836, son of John Pringle, a jeweller in Perth, and his wife Janet Cameron, died in New York on 8 June 1869. [Perth, Greyfriars, gravestone]

PRINGLE, ROBERT, born 1839, son of John Pringle, a jeweller in Perth, and his wife Janet Cameron, died in Wellington, New Zealand, on 9 December 1869. [Greyfriars gravestone, Perth]

PRINGLE, WILLIAM, born 1791, son of John Pringle a jeweller in Perth, and his wife Janet Cameron, died in Demerara in December 1815. [Perth, Greyfriars gravestone]

PRINGLE, Mrs, born 1747, spouse of Reverend Dr Pringle, died in Perth on 24 May 1820. [SM.86.190]

PROUDFOOT, GEORGE, of Balbuchty, a merchant in Perth, dead by 1855, uncle of Laurence Proudfoot a physician in New York. [NRS.S/H]

PROUDFOOT, JAMES, born 1732 in Perth, emigrated to Boston, Massachusetts, in 1754, a minister in Pennsylvania and New York from 1757 to 1799, died in Salem, N.Y., on 22 October 1802. [CCMC]

PROUDFOOT, JAMES, born 1828, son of Alexander Proudfoot and his wife Catherine Clark, settled in Canterbury, New Zealand, died on 24 April 1911. [Fortingall gravestone]

PULLAR, ALEXANDER, born 1840, son of Alexander Pullar and his wife Margaret Logie, died in Gore, New Zealand, on 18 April 1914. [Little Dunkeld gravestone]

PULLAR, JOHN, born 183-, son of Alexander Pullar and his wife Margaret Logie, died in Melbourne, Australia, on 22 July 1910. [Little Dunkeld gravestone]

PULLAR, THOMAS, born 1833, died in New Britain, Connecticut, on 3 March 1901. [Little Dunkeld gravestone]

PULLAR, WILLIAM, tenant of New Delvine, Little Dunkeld, was accused of fraud in 1819. [NRS.AD14.19.30]

RALPH, GEORGE, blacksmith and locksmith in Perth in 1795. [NRS.GD1.427.16/6]

RAMSAY, JAMES, a merchant in Perth, 1803. [NRS.CS271.581]

RAMSAY, JAMES, minister at Madderty, versus Patrick Henry, in 1811. [NRS.CS271.68653]

RANKINE, MARGARET, youngest daughter of Thomas Rankine in Perthshire, married Captain Alexander Elder of the brig St George of St John in St John, New Brunswick, on 1 June 1829. [NBC.6.6.1829]

RATTRAY, JOHN, of New Rattray, curator bonis for Miss Grace Rattray in Forfar, a deed, 1824. [NRS.GD16.42.753]

RATTRAY, ROBERT, a hatmaker, seventh son of James Rattray in Coupar Angus, died in Cincinatti, Ohio, on 14 February 1849. [SG.18.1809][W.XVIII.1809]

REEKIE, MARGARET, was found guilty of forgery in Perth in 1813, sentenced to be transported to the colonies for seven years. [NRS.GD1.959]

REID, ALEXANDER, a prisoner in Perth Tolbooth accused of sheep stealing, was sentenced to be hanged in 1820. [NRS.JC26.1820.112]

REID, EBENEZER, born 1791, a schoolmaster and wright in Innerpeffrey, Monzie, was accused of assault and sodomy in 1836. [NRS.AD14.36.402]

REID, JAMES, was accused of robbery on the road from Fowlis to Crieff in 1800. [NRS.JC26.1800.22]

REID, JOHN, born 1778, a farmer from Perthshire, with his wife Eliza born 1780, son Alexander born 1800, and daughter Ann born 1802, emigrated via Port Glasgow aboard the <u>Commerce</u> bound for Pictou, Nova Scotia, on 10 August 1803. [NLS.ms1053.104-109]

REID, ROBERT G., son of William Reid, [1818-1867], and his wife Catherine Gillespie, [1811-1909], died in Montreal, Quebec, in 1908. [Coupar Angus gravestone]

REID, Dr THOMAS, eldest son of Robert Reid a land-surveyor in Perth, died in Port Antonio, Jamaica, on 14 December 1819. [EA.5872.151]

RENNIE, THOMAS, born 1823, son of William Rennie and his wife Elizabeth Brand, died in Taradale, Australia, on 23 July 1882. [Perth, Greyfriars gravestone]

RIACH, JOHN, a schoolteacher in Perth, a letter, 1803. [PKA.B59.24.6.135]

RICHARDSON, COLIN, from Perthshire, a member of the Scots Charitable Society of Boston in 1818. [NEHGS/SCS]

RICHARDSON, JAMES, son of Patrick Richardson in Perth, a student at Marischal College, Aberdeen, in 1820s. [MCA]

RICHMOND, GEORGE, a farmer in Moneydie, a letter to John Kennedy in Newhall, 1800. [NRS.GD112.39.86.3]; failed to appear for jury service in 1811. [NRS.JC26.1811.25]

RICHMOND, JAMES, a merchant in Auchterarder, a decreet, 1831. [NRS.CS46.1831.2.30]

RICHARDSON, COLIN, from Perthshire, was admitted as a member of the Scots Charitable Society of Boston in 1818. [SCS/NEHGS]

RICHARDSON, HELEN, fourth daughter of William Richardson of Keithock, married Michael Ramsay of the Honourable East India Company, on 12 June 1820. [SM.86.94]

RICHARDSON, JAMES, of Kinnaird, a decreet, 1812. [NRS.CS40.16.57]; versus William Duncan, late tenant in Goughton, a decreet, 1814

RICHARDSON, WILLIAM, son of Patrick Richardson a merchant in Perth, a student at Marischal College, Aberdeen, in 1820s, later a surgeon in London. [MCA]

RINTOUL, PETER, a farmer in Ladywell, Auchterarder, 1848-1849. [PKA.B59.35.100]

RINTOUL, LAURENCE, from Perth, a theological student in 1812, emigrated to America. [UPC]

RINTOUL, ROBERT, born 1753, from Middleton, Kinross, emigrated to New England in 1769, settled in Salem, Massachusetts, died on 17 July 1816. [ImmNE.161]

RINTOUL, THOMAS, a sailor in Perth, dead by 1833, brother of Helen Rintoul or Kennedy in New York. [NRS.S/H]

RITCHIE, Reverend Dr DAVID, born in Perth, Rector of Roseau, Dominica, died there on 22 September 1801. [SM.64.181] [GM.72.181]

RITCHIE, or ALLPORT, ELIZABETH, in Hobart, Tasmania, in 1862. [NRS.S.C. Perth.63.27]

RITCHIE, HANNAH, widow of John Ritchie a maltman in Perth, accused of theft in 1802 but not proven. [NRS.JC11.40]

RITCHIE, JAMES, a weaver in Perth, dead by 1799, brother of William Ritchie in Baltimore, Maryland. [NRS.S/H]

RITCHIE, JAMES, tacksman of Cargill in 1811. [PKA.B59.38.5.41]

RITCHIE, JAMES ANDREW, born 31 August 1844, son of Reverend William Ritchie, [1805-1895], and his wife Margaret Brown, [1819-1898], died in Chicago, Illinois, on 11 July 1879. [Longforgan gravestone]

RITCHIE, PETER, a distiller in Strowan, sequestration, 1808. [NRS.CS236.R12.2]

RITCHIE, THOMAS, born 1827, fourth son of Thomas Ritchie a farmer in Evelick, Perthshire, a merchant in Jacksonville, Florida, died there on 12 May 1877. [EC.28921]

RITCHIE, WILLIAM, in Baltimore, Maryland, brother and heir of James Ritchie a weaver in Perth, 1799. [NRS.S/H]

ROB, JOHN, in Dunblane, 1812. [NRS.CS313.1024]

ROBERTSON, ALEXANDER, born 1771, a labourer from Fortingall, with his wife Catherine born 1777, aboard the <u>Clarendon of Hull</u> bound for Prince Edward Island, Canada, in August 1808. [NSARM][TNA.CO226.23]

ROBERTSON, ALEXANDER, of Strowan, husband of Jean Stewart, probate 1830, Prerogative Court of Canterbury. [TNA] [NRS.GD2.15.48]

ROBERTSON, ALEXANDER, born 1837, son of James Robertson, a blacksmith in Errol, and his wife Helen Sandeman, died in New South Wales, Australia, on 10 October 1873. [Errol gravestone]

ROBERTSON, ANN, wife of Thomas Gardner in Perth, died on 3 December 1857. [NRS.S/H]

ROBERTSON, BARBARA, born 1779 in Perthshire, widow of Charles Duff, emigrated to New Brunswick in 1801, died at St Mary's, Nashwaak, N.B., on 8 April 1836. [NB Royal Gazette, 13.4.1836]

ROBERTSON, CHARLES, from Kincarnie, emigrated via Liverpool to North America in June 1833. [SG.2.152]

ROBERTSON, DANIEL, born 1774 in Perthshire, emigrated to New Brunswick around 1816, died at Loch Lomond, St John, N.B., on 28 December 1843. [New Brunswick Courier, 30.12.1843]

ROBERTSON, DAVID, in Crieff, was a victim of robbery on the road from Fowlis to Crieff in 1800. [NRS.JC26.1800.22]

ROBERTSON, DAVID, born 1829, son of David Robertson and his wife Helen Malloch in Perth, died in Natal, South Africa, in February 1878. [Perth Greyfriars gravestone]

ROBERTSON, DAVID, born 1834, son of Robert Robertson and his wife Janet Kennedy, died in Chicago, Illinois, on 3 March 1871. [Logerait gravestone]

ROBERTSON, DONALD, in Lochearnhead, applied to operate the inn at Killin in 1807. [NRS.GD112.11.7.8.1.11]

ROBERTSON, DONALD, with his wife Catherine, from Dull, emigrated via Greenock aboard the <u>Curlew</u> bound for Quebec on 21 July 1818. [TNA.CO384/3.123-127]

ROBERTSON, DONALD, with his wife Janet, from Dull, emigrated via Greenock aboard the <u>Curlew</u> bound for Quebec on 21 July 1818. [TNA.CO384/3.123-127]

ROBERTSON, DUNCAN, in Calvine, Blair Atholl, a prisoner in Perth Tolbooth, accused of sheep stealing in 1801. [NRS.JC26.1801.13]

ROBERTSON, DUNCAN, born 1761, a farmer from Perthshire, with his wife Isabella born 1772, son Alexander born 1797, daughter Eliza born 1799, daughter Margaret born 1802, and daughter Isabella born 1803, emigrated via Port Glasgow aboard the <u>Commerce</u> bound for Pictou, Nova Scotia, on 10 August 1803. [NLS.ms1053.104-109]

ROBERTSON, DUNCAN, born 1787, a labourer from Strathbraan, emigrated aboard the <u>Clarendon of Hull</u> bound for Prince Edward Island in August 1808. [NSARM] [TNA.CO226.23]

ROBERTSON, DUNCAN, born 21 October 1781, son of Reverend James Robertson and his wife Isabella Graham in Callander, emigrated to Jamaica. [F.4.340]

ROBERTSON, DUNCAN, with his wife Margaret and two children, from Dull, emigrated via Greenock aboard the <u>Curlew</u> bound for Quebec on 21 July 1818. [TNA.CO384/3.123-127]

ROBERTSON, ELIZABETH, from Kincarnie, emigrated via Liverpool to North America in June 1833. [SG.2.152]

ROBERTSON, GEORGE, of Struan, died 3 April 1864, uncle of Alexander Gilbert Robertson of Struan in Jamaica. [NRS.S/H]

ROBERTSON, GEORGINA, eldest daughter of Major Robertson of Cray, Perthshire, married William Guild jr., a merchant in Montreal, in Quebec on 29 July 1829. [SM.26.841][BM.26.841]

ROBERTSON, HENRY, son of Reverend James Robertson in Callander, a student in Marischal College, graduated MA in 1795. [MCA]

ROBERTSON, HOPE FLEMING, born 1825, second son of John Robertson and his wife Susan Fleming, in Laigh of Cluny, Strathtay, died on 28 November 1883 in St Louis, USA. [Logerait gravestone] [S.12362]

ROBERTSON, HUGH, born 1791 in Perthshire, emigrated via Greenock to New York, was naturalised there on 17 April 1821. [NARA]

ROBERTSON, JAMES, born 1729, a labourer from Fortingall, emigrated, with his wife Catherine born 1737, aboard the Clarendon of Hull bound for Prince Edward Island in August 1808. [NSARM][TNA.CO226.23]

ROBERTSON, JAMES, born 1775 in Perthshire, died in Charleston, South Carolina, on 14 May 1809. [Old Scots gravestone, Charleston]

ROBERTSON, JAMES, born 1784, a labourer from Strathbraan, emigrated aboard the Clarendon of Hull bound for Prince Edward Island, Canada, in August 1808. [NSARM] [TNA.CO226.23]

ROBERTSON, JAMES, in Tombane, Blair Atholl, accused of assault in 1827. [NRS.AD14.27.297]

ROBERTSON, JAMES, from Perth, graduated MA from King's College, Aberdeen, in March 1826, later a Free Church minister in Wilmot, Nova Scotia. [KCA]

ROBERTSON, JAMES, born 1791 in Perthshire, a grocer in Charleston, South Carolina, was naturalised on 13 October 1834. [NARA.M1181]

ROBERTSON, JAMES, MD, FRCSE, born 1825 in Dunkeld, died in Alexandria, Virginia, on 21 July 1866. [DA.1673]

ROBERTSON, JAMES, born 1825, son of John Robertson, [1790-1849], and his wife Janet Small, [1793-1859], died in Arthur, America, on 18 September 1883. [Rattray gravestone]

ROBERTSON, JOHN, son of John Robertson, a farmer, [1765-1837], and his wife Margaret Robertson, [1776-1848], a Senator of the Dominion of Canada. [Dowally gravestone]

ROBERTSON, JOHN DUFF, son of John Robertson a weaver in Perth, was apprenticed to James Moncreiff a brassfounder in Perth for five years in 1812. [NRS.GD1.427.16/12]

ROBERTSON, JOHN, from Blair Atholl, emigrated via Greenock aboard the Curlew bound for Quebec on 21 July 1818. [TNA.CO384/3.123-127]

ROBERTSON, JOHN, with his wife Catherine, from Dull, emigrated via Greenock aboard the Curlew bound for Quebec on 21 July 1818. [TNA.CO384/3.123-127]

ROBERTSON, JOHN, with his wife Janet and two children, from Killin, emigrated via Greenock aboard the <u>Curlew</u> bound for Quebec on 21 July 1818. [TNA.CO384/3.123-127]

ROBERTSON, JOHN, tenant farmer in the Wood of Murie, accused of theft in 1831. [NRS.AD14.31.55]

ROBERTSON, JOHN, son of Francis Robertson in Perth, a student at Marischal College, Aberdeen, in the 1830s, an Advocate in Aberdeen in 1852. [MCA]

ROBERTSON, JOHN, born 1769, died in Milton, Perthshire, on 6 August 1837. [New Brunswick Courier.28.10.1837]

ROBERTSON, JOHN, was found guilty of forgery in Perth in 1815 and sentenced to seven years transportation to the colonies. [NRS.GD1.959]

ROBERTSON, JOHN, born 1812, of Path of Condie, was accused of housebreaking and theft in 1835. [NRS.AD14.35.108]

ROBERTSON, JOHN, guilty of housebreaking and theft, was sentenced to transportation to the colonies for seven years, at Perth in April 1832. [PKA.B59.26.11.3.6]

ROBERTSON, JOHN, born 1823, son of David Robertson and his wife Helen Malloch, died in Florida in 1878. [Perth, Greyfriars, gravestone]

ROBERTSON, JOHN, in Pitlochry, father of John Robertson, born 1872, was killed at the Shangani River, Matabeleland, on 4 February 1898. [Moulin gravestone]

ROBERTSON, JOSEPH, session clerk of Dunblane Free Church a petition, 1845. [NRS.GD112.51.189]

ROBERTSON, KATHERINE MAY ANN LINDSAY, sixth daughter of Major Robertson of Craig, married John Walker from Honduras, in Craig House, Perthshire, on 1 July 1851. [AJ.5400]

ROBERTSON, MARGARET, daughter of Peter Robertson in Abernethy, a victim of crime in 1823. [NRS.JCC26.1823.198]

ROBERTSON, MARJORIE, born 1820, daughter of Andrew Robertson, a brewer in Longforgan, wife of R. Christie, died in Melbourne, Victoria, Australia, on 19 December 1866. [Longforgan gravestone]

ROBERTSON, or SULLIVAN, MARY, in Perth Tolbooth, accused of theft in 1816. [NRS.JC26.1816.139]

ROBERTSON, MARY, born 1825, daughter of David Robertson and his wife Helen Malloch, died in Melbourne, Australia, in April 1859. [Perth Greyfriars gravestone]

ROBERTSON, PETER, from Dull, emigrated via Greenock aboard the Curlew bound for Quebec on 21 July 1818. [TNA.CO384/3.123-127]

ROBERTSON, ROBERT, accused of debauchery in Abernethy, was outlawed in 1823. [NRS.JC26.1823.198]

ROBERTSON, ROBERT S., chairman of the Blair Atholl Free Church, a letter, 1845. [NRS.GD112.51.186]

ROBERTSON, THOMAS, and the trustees of Scone Burgher Congregation, versus James Wylie in 1812. [NRS.CS42.4.126]

ROBERTSON, WILLIAM, born 1803, son of David Robertson and his wife Helen Malloch, died in Chicago, Illinois, in March 1877. [Perth, Greyfriars gravestone]

ROBERTSON, WILLIAM, born 1804, a mason in Rattray, accused of assault in 1828. [NRS.AD14.26.159]

ROBERTSON, WILLIAM, MD, son of William Robertson in Perth, married Mary Elizabeth Tierney, eldest daughter of B. Tierney, the Customs Controller, in Corillon, Upper Canada, on 6 April 1838. [AJ.4726]

ROBERTSON, WILLIAM, of Bridge Farm, Blairgowrie, a cattle dealer, ship owner and trader, 1842. [NRS.CS280.17.17]

ROBEY, Mrs JANET, born 1779 in Perthshire, wife of George Robey a dyer, emigrated via Dundee, naturalised in New York on 20 April 1822. [NY Court of Common Pleas]

ROBIN, DANIEL, a mason in Dalquiech, Orwell, son of Christian Robertson or Robin, was accused of sheep stealing in 1832. [NRS.AD14.32.171]

ROBIN, JEAN, born 1804, a sewer in Dunblane, was accused of child murder in 1826. [NRS.AD14.26.160]

ROBINSON, SAMUEL, in Precinct Street, Coupar Angus, a victim of theft in 1829. [NRS.AC14.29.128]

ROGER, JOHN, from Muckhart, Kinross, a theological student in 1765, a missionary in America in 1770, later a minister in Pennsylvania. [UPC]

ROGERS, Reverend JOHN, minister of Collace later minister of the Scotch Church in Madras, India, in 1830. [NRS.GD51.4.1685]

ROLLO, ALEXANDER, in Tofthill, Inchyra, Kinnoul, was accused of fraud and perjury, and was outlawed in 1806. [NRS.JC11.48]

ROSS, ALEXANDER, born 1756, son of Alexander Ross, [1712-1785], and his wife Catherine Rutherford, [1711-1785], died in New York on 26 December 1805. [Kinnoull gravestone]

ROSS, DAVID, a tenant in Manorleys, Portmoak, Kinross, in America by 1818. [NRS.CS17.1.38/363]

ROSS, JAMES, a weaver in Dunning, died 13 November 1868, father of James Ross in Salt Lake, Utah. [NRS.S/H]

ROSS, MARY, a crockery dealer, was sentenced to transportation to the colonies for fourteen years, at Perth on 16 April 1829. [NRS.B59.26.11.3]

ROSS, WILLIAM, a farmer in Lairwell later in Perth, died 19 June 1854, father of David Ross in New South Wales, Australia. [NRS.S/H]

ROSS, ....., emigrated from Perth aboard the <u>Atlantic of Perth</u> in April 1840, was shipwrecked off Cape Francois, Canada, on 5 May 1840, but was saved. [EEC.20062]

ROY, or SOUTAR, Mrs MARGARET, in Methven a disposition, 1844. [PKA.B59.40.284]

RUSSELL, JAMES, from Dunblane, a theological student in 1816, emigrated to America. [UPC]

RUSSELL, Dr JAMES, minister in Dunning, versus Jess Scott in 1824. [NRS.CS271.57317]

RUTHERFORD, ALEXANDER, from Perthshire, died in Montreal or Quebec on 16 June 1832. [GA.4258].

RUTHERFORD, JAMES, born 1819 in Crieff, a distiller in New York, died 14 February 1903. [ANY]

RUTHERFORD, PETER, a builder in Aberfeldy, petitioned for land, there in 1808. [NRS.GD112.11.8.4.5]

SAGE, J., born 1832 in Perth, son of William Sage and his wife Susan, a physician who settled in Jefferson County, Georgia, by 1850. [Perth, Greyfriars, gravestone]

SANDEMAN, HUGH, born 1830, fourth son of Glas Sandeman and his wife Margaret Stewart of Bonskeid, died in Buenos Ayres, Argentina, on 20 December 1854. [Perth Greyfriars gravestone] [EEC.22715]

SANDEMAN, JOHN, born 6 April 1809 in Redgorton, son of William John Sandeman, a bleacher in Luncarty, and his wife Elizabeth Steuart, to India in 1828, a Lieutenant of the Bengal Army, died at Landur on 20 January 1841. [BA.4.12]

SANDEMAN, ROBERT TURNBULL, born 1 October 1804 in Perth, son of William Sandeman and his wife Catherine Turnbull, to India in 1825, Major General of the 33$^{rd}$ Native Infantry of the Bengal Army, died in London on 25 July 1876. [BA.4.12]

SANDEMAN, WILLIAM ROBERT, born 1820, son of Hector Sandeman and his wife Catherine Turnbull, died in Sydney, Australia, on 21 December 1841. [Perth Greyfriars gravestone]

SANDERS, WILLIAM, in Perth, died 17 September 1860, cousin of William Blair Sanders, a merchant in Toronto, Canada. [NRS.S/H.1876]

SCOBIE, JOHN, alias Roger MacLeish, in Newton of Pitcairn, Dunning, accused of assault, in 1820, trial papers. [NRS.JC26.1820.19]

SCOTT, ALEXANDER, labourer in Drum, Kellyburn, Muckart, in 1827, accused of housebreaking and theft in 1827, outlawed. [NRS.AD14.27.168; JC26.1827.168]

SCOTT, COLIN PATRICK, second son of Reverend John Scott in Muthill, died in Antigua in June 1794. [EA.3209.214][SM.56.588]

SCOTT, JAMES, born 14 October 1792, in Kinclaven, son of Reverend John Scott and his wife Ann Swan, Captain of the British Legion in Columbian Service, was killed at the Battle of Carabobo in South America on 24 June 1821. [F.4.163]

SCOTT, JAMES MUIR, MD, grandson of Reverend Scott in Perth, died in Waterford, Virginia, on 20 September 1821. [SM.89.559]

SCOTT, JOHN, from Perthshire, a student at Haldane's Seminary in Edinburgh, a Baptist, settled on the North River, Prince Edward Island, Canada, in 1806. [ST]

SCOTT, JOHN, with his wife Margaret, from Dull, emigrated via Greenock aboard the Curlew bound for Quebec on 21 July 1818. [TNA.CO384/3.123-127]

SCOTT, JOHN, born 1813, an apprentice tanner in Dunning, accused of poaching in 1832. [NRS.AD14.32.97]

SCOTT, JOHN, in Millhaugh of Dunning, 1841. [NRS.CS279.2515]

SCOTT, MARGARET, daughter of Reverend John Scott in Kinclaven, widow of Dr Power in St John, Newfoundland, married John Cooper from Dalmeny, in Dundee on 26 January 1821. [EA.5966.71]

SCOTT, MARGARET ESTHER, born 1804, a thief and a prostitute, was sentenced to transportation to the colonies, at Perth on 18 September 1833. [NRS.B59.26.11.3]

SCOTT, PATRICK, in Aberfeldy, petitioned to build a house in the Square of Aberfeldy in 1807. [NRS.GD112.11.8.1.15]

SCOTT, ROBERT, with his wife Margaret and one child, from Dull, emigrated via Greenock aboard the Curlew bound for Quebec on 21 July 1818. [TNA.CO384/3.123-127]

SCOTT, ROBERT, with his wife Nelly, from Dull, emigrated via Greenock aboard the Curlew bound for Quebec on 21 July 1818. [TNA.CO384/3.123-127]

SCOTT, ROBERT, labourer in Drum, Kellyburn, Muckart, in 1827, accused of housebreaking and theft in 1827, was outlawed. [NRS.AD14.27.168; JC26.1827.168]

SCOTT, THOMAS, born 1746, eldest son of Reverend Alexander Scott and his wife Euphan Henderson, the Chief Justice of Canada, died in 1824. [Meigle gravestone]

SCOTT, WILLIAM, tenant in Dron, sederunt book, 1795-1811. [NRS.CS96.4367]

SCOTT, WILLIAM, born 1783, a labourer from Strathbraan, emigrated aboard the Clarendon of Hull bound for Prince Edward Island, Canada, in August 1808. [NSARM] [TNA.CO226.23]

SCOTT, WILLIAM, born 1825, son of Robert Scott and his wife Margaret McKechnie, died on 17 February 1860 in Sydney, Australia. [Perth Greyfriars gravestone]

SCOTT, Captain, master of the Queen of Perth from Dundee to Australia in 1853, landed in Melbourne, Australia, on 21 September 1853. [AJ.5527]

SCRIMGEOUR, ROBERT, born 1802, in Hillyland, Perth, a print-cutter with Mr Peacock, South Methven Street, Perth, was accused of breach of trust and embezzlement in 1849. [NRS.AD14.49.93]

SCRIMGEOUR, ROBERT, son of James Scrimgeour a shoemaker in Perth, was educated at Marischal College, Aberdeen, in 1846. [MCA]

SCRIMGEOUR, WILLIAM, born 23 February 1807 in Perth, emigrated to New York in 1836, died in Brooklyn on 10 June 1885. [ANY]

SHANKLING, GEORGE, guilty of theft, was sentenced to transportation to the colonies for fourteen years, at Perth in 1829. [NRS.B59.26.11.3]

SHAW, DAVID, a farmer from Strone of Cully, Blairgowrie, in Colorado by 1871. [NRS.RS.Forfar.26.253]

SHAW, JAMES, born 1822 in Abernethy, a store-keeper in Charleston, South Carolina, was naturalised on 5 April 1853. [NARA.M11831]

SHAW, JOSEPH, born 1778 in Rattray, son of James Shaw and his wife Ann Paterson, was educated at Edinburgh University, a theological student in Edinburgh in 1794, emigrated to Philadelphia in 1805, a minister and academic in Albany Academy, New York and in Dickenson College, Carlisle, Pennsylvania, died in Philadelphia, Pennsylvania, on 21 August 1824. [AP][UPC]

SHEDDAN, JOHN, a baker in Perth, dead by 1788, father of John Sheddan in Abingdon, North America. [NRS.S/H]

SHEPHERD, CATHERINE, wife of Alexander Weepers in Couper Angus, accused of theft and assault in 1812. [NRS.AD14.12.50]

SHEPHERD, THOMAS, born 1792 in Perth, son of John Shepherd and his wife Ann Jamieson, a merchant in New York, died there on 7 March 1854. [ANY]

SHERWOOD, GEORGE, son of George Sherwood a shoemaker in Perth, was educated at Marischal College in 1842, later a minister at Sheuchan. [MCA]

SHORTHOUSE, JOHN, a cattle dealer on Gallowhill, Kinross, was accused of assault and robbery in 1834. [NRS.AD14.34.19]

SHORTHOUSE, ROBERT, born 1812, son of Robert Shorthouse, a miner on Kinross Muir accused of assault and robbery in 1834. [NRS.AD14.34.19]

SIMPSON, ALEXANDER KERR, born 28 June 1829, son of Kerr Simpson on Hill of Gourdie, [1779-1867], and his wife Margaret Angus, [1789-1836], of the Indian Medical Service, died in Suakin, South Africa, on 17 August 1859. [Clunie gravestone]

SIMPSON, PATRICK, from Perth, settled on John's Island, South Carolina, testament, 1794, Comm. Edinburgh. [NRS]

SIMPSON, ROBERT, in Nether Durdie, Kilspindale, a victim of sheep stealing in 1837. [NRS.AD14.37.386]

SIMPSON, WILLIAM, in Milnathort, Kinross, victim of a shooting and assault in 1829. [NRS.AD14.29.307]

SINCLAIR, ALEXANDER, from Perthshire, was naturalised in South Carolina on 10 January 1804. [S.C. Common Plea Court.3.232]

SINCLAIR, ALEXANDER, born 1780, a merchant from Little Faudie, sometime Adjutant of the Breadalbane Fencibles, settled in Charleston, South Carolina, by 1808, died on 1 August 1838. [SG.722] [Old Scots gravestone, Charleston]

SINCLAIR, ALEXANDER, born 1793 in Perthshire, son of Donald Sinclair, husband of Christina McLaren, 1809-1879, settled in Maxville, Glengarry County, Ontario, died in 1841. [CGS.64]

SINCLAIR, ARCHIBALD, a mason in Blairgowrie, was accused of forgery in 1831. [NRS.AD14.31.376]

SINCLAIR, CATHERINE, in Little Comrie, Weem, having charge of 86 years old Margaret McGregor, petitioned for aid in 1831. [NRS.GD112.11.9.7.91]

SINCLAIR, FINLAY, born 1792 in Perthshire, son of Donald Sinclair, husband of Mary McLaren, 1797-1870, settled in Glengarry County, Ontario, died in 1869. [CGS.64]

SINCLAIR, JOHN, son of D. Sinclair in Kinloch Rannoch, an assistant surgeon on HMS Pylades died in Jamaica in August 1825. [BM.18.779]

SKENE, WILLIAM, son of William Skene a carpenter in Taymouth, who died in 1856, and his wife Isabella MacLoorie, 1786-1834, died in Belize, Honduras, during 1848. [Kenmore gravestone]

SKINNER, GEORGE URE, born 1805, second son of the Very Reverend John Skinner the Dean of Dunkeld and Dunblane, settled in Guatamala, died in Aspinwall, Panama, on 9 February 1862. [AJ.6215] [S.7342]

SMART, DAVID, in Middleton of Collinoqhies, Orwell, Kinross, a victim of housebreaking in 1837. [NRS.AD14.37.200]

SMEATON, THOMAS WRIGHT, born 15 May 1859, son of Reverend John Smeaton and his wife Mary Drummond Wright, died in Canada on 17 August 1909. [Auchterarder gravestone]

SMITH, ANN, in Drum of Garvock, Dunning, a victim of housebreaking in 1836. [NRS.AD14.36.77]

SMITH, DAVID, in Blairgowrie, a victim of forgery in 1824. [NRS.AD14.24.101]

SMITH, DONALD, born 1762 in Perthshire, died 9 June 1843, husband of Jennet McIntosh. [Creighton Cemetery, Upper Mount Thom, Pictou County, NS]

SMITH, ELIZABETH, born 1798 in Perthshire, died 15 September 1856, wife of Donald Munroe. [Creighton Cemetery, Upper Mount Thom, Pictou County, NS]

SMITH, JAMES, from Methven, a theological student in 1819, graduated DD, a minister at Steviacke, Nova Scotia, later a Professor of Biblical Literature. [UPC]

SMITH, JAMES, born 1825 in Fowlis Wester, son of Thomas Smith a tailor, was educated at Glasgow University, a minister in Argentina from 1850, died on 9 October 1906. [F.7.683]

SMITH, JANET, in Drum of Garvock, Dunning, a victim of housebreaking in 1836. [NRS.AD14.36.77]

SMITH, JOHN, in Drum of Garvock, Dunning, a victim of housebreaking in 1836. [NRS.AD14.36.77]

SMITH, JOHN, tenant in Haughs of Kinnaird, and Margaret Brand Neill, daughter of David Neill tenant in the Mans of Ardestie, Angus, a marriage contract, sederunt book, 1848. [NRS.CS96.4873]

SMITH, MARY, in Drummond Lodge, Callendar, married Peter, William Wallace, MD, of the Royal Naval Hospital, Esquimalt, Vancouver Island, British Columbia, there on 20 January 1862. [S.2106]

SMYLES, ELIZABETH, born 1809, widow of Alexander Kinleyside a teacher in Coupar Angus, died in Rochester, New York, on 24 April 1875. [S.9924]

SMYTHE, GEORGE, of Methven, died 1834, letters. [NRS.GD190.3.342]

SMYTH, ROBERT, of Methven, versus Reverend William Liston in 1816. [NRS.CS40.22.53]

SOMERVILLE, ANDREW, born 1781, son of Robert Somerville and his wife Isabel Scotland, from Kenmore, with his wife Janet Buchanan, born 1791, and son John born 1813, emigrated via Port Glasgow aboard the Favourite of St John bound for St John, New Brunswick, on 22 October 1815. [PANB.ms.RS23E.fo.9798]

SORLEY, JAMES, in Ramayle of Dunblane, versus David Crawford, tenant of Hutchesontown, 1803. [NRS.CC271.642]

SPENCE, DAVID, born 1811, a labourer in Errol, accused of robbery in 1841. [NRS.AD14.41.154]

SPENCE, PATRICK, minister of Orwell, Kinross, letters 1792-1800. [NRS.GD29.154]

SPIERS, JOHN, born 1835, son of John W. Spiers, [1809-1879], died in Barawy, Ba Coast, Fiji, on 1 July 1871. [Caputh gravestone]

SPIERS, ROBERT, born 1837, son of John W. Spiers, [1809-1879], died in Sydney, Australia, on 20 October 1895. [Caputh gravestone]

SPINDLER, GEORGE, a grocer in Errol, a victim of housebreaking and theft in 1820. [NRS.JC26.1820.10]

SPOTISWOOD, DUNCAN, cashier of the Perth Banking Company, versus William Thom a merchant in Blairgowrie, 1816. [NRS.CS40.22.95]

STALKER, DUNCAN, born 1782, son of Daniel Stalker a merchant in Comrie, was educated at Glasgow University in 1799, a minister in Peebles from 1807 until 1830, then a minister in New Argyle, Washington County, New York, from 1831 until his death on 5 December 1853. [MAGU][PC.1.572]

STEEDMAN, DAVID, in Kinross, a victim of forgery in 1831. [NRS.AD14.31.376]

STEEDMAN, JOHN, petitioned to erect a stone at the grave of his daughter Margaret in Greyfriars, Perth, in 1806. [PKA.B59.24.5.12]

STEVENS, AGNES, born 1855, daughter of James Stevens and his wife Ann Dron, wife of James Thomson, died in Sydney, Australia, on 15 February 1934. [Kinross, Kirkgate gravestone]

STEVENS, CHARLES, born 1858, son of James Stevens and his wife Ann Dron, died in New Zealand on 6 October 1940. [Kinross, Kirkgate gravestone]

STEVENS, JOHN, born 1839, son of James Stevens and his wife Ann Dron, died in Dunedin, New Zealand in 1895. [Kinross, Kirkgate gravestone]

STEVENSON, JAMES, a merchant and banker in Dunkeld, trustee of John Stewart, 1819. [NRS.CS36.26.36]

STEWART, ALEXANDER, formerly a merchant at the Bridge of Tilt, by 1795 in the West Indies. [NRS.CS17.1.14/247]

STEWART, ALEXANDER, a tenant farmer at Pitkerral, Bridge of Dull, dead by 1798, father of John Stewart in Albany, New York. [NRS.S/H]

STEWART, ALEXANDER, a tenant from Blair Atholl, emigrated via Fort William aboard the Dove bound for Pictou, Nova Scotia, in June 1801. [NRS.RH2.4.87.73-75]

STEWART, ALEXANDER, with his wife Margaret, from Blair Atholl, emigrated via Greenock aboard the Curlew bound for Quebec on 21 July 1818. [TNA.CO384/3.123-127]

STEWART, ALEXANDER, tenant in Stroan, Callander, accused of homicide in 1820. [NRS.AD14.20.252]

STEWART, ALEXANDER, a butcher in Perth, accused of sheep stealing in 1825. [NRS.JC26.1825.295]

STEWART, MALCOLM ALEXANDER, son of Malcolm Stewart of Athole Bank, Perthshire, died in Edinburgh on 29 November 1825. [SM.97.127]

STEWART, ALEXANDER, son of James Stewart, [1800-1872], and his wife Annie McLaren, [1808-1894], died in Port Lavaco, America, in 1897. [Blair Atholl gravestone]

STEWART, ALEXANDER, footman to Archibald Douglas in Clan Gregor Castle, Kilmadock, was accused of housebreaking in 1835. [NRS.AD14.35.115]

STEWART, ANDREW DAVID, born 3 September 1813, son of James Alston Stewart, [1763-1833], and his wife Charlotte Stewart, [1780-1837], died in Missouri on 17 May 1848. [Moulin gravestone]

STEWART, ANGUS, a chapman from Kencroak, Glen Lyon, in America by 1795. [NRS.CS17.1.14/247]

STEWART, ANGUS, born 1792 in Perthshire, an innkeeper in Charleston, South Carolina, was naturalised there on 4 October 1832. [NARA.M1183.1]

STEWART, ANN, a tinker, was sentenced to transportation to the colonies for fourteen years, in Perth on 16 April 1829. [PKA.B59.26.11.3]

STEWART, CHARLES, married Ann Nicholson in Dull on 7 October 1780, emigrated with their children Isabel, John, Donald, Alexander, Charles, James, Catherine, Jennie, and Malcolm, to Prince Edward Island, Canada, in 1804. [SG]

STEWART, CHARLES, born in Perth, settled in New York, died in Georgia on 12 August 1800. [Georgia gravestone] [Colonial Museum and Savanna Advertiser, 15.8.1800]

STEWART, CHARLES, born 1794, a labourer from Aberfeldy, emigrated aboard the Clarendon of Hull bound for Prince Edward Island in August 1808. [NSARM] [TNA.CO226.23]

STEWART, CHARLES, of the Free Presbytery of Dunkeld, a petition, 1845. [NRS.GD1.2.51.178]

STEWART, CHARLES C., minister of the Free Church in Dunning, a letter, 1845. [NRS.GD112.51.186]

STEWART, DANIEL, born 1803, sometime of Cayuka, Hamilton, Canada, died 31 October 1883. [Dunblane gravestone]

STEWART, DANIEL, born 1833 in Croft Douglas, Perthshire, died in Canada on 27 September 1925; husband of Catherine McNabb, born 1855, died 1 September 1925. [White Lake Community cemetery, Renfrew County, Ontario, gravestone]

STEWART, DAVID, born 7 August 1810 in Auchterarder, a merchant and insurance company director in New York, died in the Hotel Champlain on 17 July 1891. [ANY]

STEWART, DAVID, with his wife Catherine and two children, from Muthill, emigrated via Greenock aboard the Curlew bound for Quebec on 21 July 1818. [TNA.CO384/3.1236.41.1097]

STEWART, Major General DAVID, of Garth, Governor of St Lucia, died in December 1829. [NRS.GD2.147]

STEWART, DAVID, guilty of theft, was sentenced to transportation for fourteen years in 1829. [PKA.B59.26.11.3]

STEWART, DAVID OGILVIE, petitioned to open a grocer's shop in Kinnaird in 1835. [NRS.GD1]

STEWART, DONALD, born 1784, a labourer from Blair, emigrated aboard the Clarendon of Hull bound for Prince Edward Island in August 1808. [NSARM] [TNA.CO226.23]

STEWART, DONALD, born 1790, a labourer from Atholl, emigrated aboard the Clarendon of Hull bound for Prince Edward Island in August 1808. [NSARM] [TNA.CO226.23]

STEWART, DONALD, born 1793 in Perthshire, died 3 April 1855. North Lochaber cemetery, Antigonish County, NS]

STEWART, DONALD, in Wester Balvair, Blair Atholl, accused of theft in 1825. [NRS.JC26.1825.295]

STEWART, DONALD, in Dunkeld, was accused of assault in 1829. [NRS.AD14.29.141]

STEWART, DONALD, a farm servant at Bridge of Tilt, Blair Atholl, accused of sheep stealing in 1837. [NRS.AD14.37.386]

STEWART, DUNCAN, in Pitlochry, father of Mungo Stewart who died at his brother's house in Zavala, Texas, on 28 August 1876. [S.10344][AJ.6715]

STEWART, EDWARD, a servant in Blairgowrie, versus William Stewart in America, 1827. [NRS.CS46.1837.7.103]

STEWART, FRANCIS ARCHIBALD, of the 1st West India Regiment, eldest son of A. F. Stewart in Aberfoyle, Perthshire, married Grace Jane Malloch, daughter of George Malloch, in Brockville, Canada, on 10 November 1870. [S.8527]

STEWART, GEORGE, servant of Reverend John Kirk in Glendevon, a victim of assault in 1822. [NRS.AD14.22.58]

STEWART, GEORGE MURRAY, in Australia, son and heir of Dr John Stewart and his wife Helen Glass in Blair Atholl, 1853. [NRS.S/H]

STEWART, ISABELLA, from Perthshire, married George Robson late of the Royal American Artillery, in St John, New Brunswick, on 18 July 1819. [New Brunswick Courier, 24.7.1819]

STEWART, JAMES, born 1766, a farmer from Perthshire, with his wife Jane born 1766, son Donald born 1792, daughter Isabella born 1794, daughter Janet born 1796, and son Charles born 1802, emigrated via Port Glasgow aboard the Commerce bound for Pictou, Nova Scotia, on 10 August 1803. [NLS.ms1053.104-109]

STEWART, JAMES, in Dowally, factor to the Duke of Atholl, a letter to William Stewart of Ardvorlich, 1787. [NRS.GD112.167.1/19]

STEWART, JAMES, a millwright in St Thomas in the East, Jamaica, appointed William Stewart of Ardvorlich, Comrie, as his attorney in 1792, reference to his brother John Stewart late of the East India Company in India. [NRS.RD3.256.777]

STEWART, JAMES, a carter between Perth and Dunkeld, accused of assault in 1821. [NRS.AD14.21.89]

STEWART, JAMES, from Jamaica, died in Perth on 2 February 1823. [DPCA.1076]

STEWART, JAMES GILLESPIE, born 29 September 1813 in Blair Atholl, son of Reverend John Stewart and his wife Ann Wight, died in Greenpark, Falmouth, Jamaica, on 23 August 1851. [F.IV.145] [ Green Park gravestone, Jamaica]

STEWART, JAMES, second son of James Stewart of Persie, residing in Dowally, died in Valparaiso, Chile, on 11 April 1822. [DPCA.1066][S.311.7]

STEWART, JAMES, born 1802 in Perthshire, died 17 June 1874. [North Lochaber cemetery, Antigonish County, NS]

STEWART, JAMES, in Shemerboun, Strathtummel, was murdered in 1837. [NRS.AD14.37.162]

STEWART, JAMES, in Cultalonie, a victim of assault in 1845. [NRS.AD14.45.291]

STEWART, JAMES, born 1843, son of David Stewart in Spittalfield, [1812-1872], and his wife Margaret Duncan, [1816-1885], died in Saginaw, USA on 17 June 1891. [Caputh gravestone]

STEWART, JAMES, son of John Stewart, [1800-1872], and his wife Annie McLaren, [1808-1894], died in Dunedin, New Zealand, in 1898. [Alyth gravestone][Blair Atholl gravestone]

STEWART, JANE, ANN, and ELIZABETH, of Bohalie, a tack of fishing on Loch Tummel in 1803. [NRS.GD132.538]

STEWART, Mrs JANET, from Killin, emigrated via Greenock aboard the Curlew bound for Quebec on 21 July 1818. [TNA.CO384/3.123-127]

STEWART, or MCCULLOCH, JOHN, a militia rioter at Castle Menzies, was sentenced to transportation to the colonies for seven years, at Perth on 7 May 1798. [AJ.2627]

STEWART, JOHN, in Cuill of Balquhidder, a bond of caution for John Stuart in Tulloch of Balquhidder in 1800. [NRS.CS271.344]

STEWART, JOHN, born 1798 in Blair Atholl, an employee of the Hudson Bay Company from 1816 to 1824, returned to Scotland. [HBRS.II.459]

STEWART, JOHN, in Strathgray, Blair Atholl, uncle and executor of Thomas McLaren a planter in Demerara, testament, 1814. [NRS.RD5.182.697]

STEWART, JOHN, with his wife Elizabeth, from Dull, emigrated via Greenock aboard the Curlew bound for Quebec on 21 July 1818. [TNA.CO384/3.123-127]

STEWART, JOHN, a weaver in Dunkeld, accused of assault in 1820. [NRS.AD14.20.143]; a weaver in Dunkeld, was accused of assault in 1822. [NRS.AD14.22.10]

STEWART, JOHN, with his wife Ellen and one child, from Blair Atholl, emigrated via Greenock aboard the Curlew bound for Quebec on 21 July 1818. [TNA.CO384/3.123-127]

STEWART, JOHN, from Garth, Perthshire, died in Garth, Trinidad, on 28 March 1830. [BM.28.571]

STEWART, Reverend JOHN, in Blair Atholl, versus David Lyon, 1831. [NRS.GD174.684]

STEWART, JOHN, a wood-ranger at Cally near Caputh, was accused of the murder of Christine Stewart his wife in 1833. [NRS.AD14.33.4]

STEWART, JOHN, born in April 1800 in Little Dunkeld, was educated at the University of Edinburgh, a minister in Nova Scotia from 1835 until his death in April 1880. [F.7.618]

STEWART, JOHN, born 1832, son of Donald Stewart and his wife Catherine McGregor, died in Ballarat, Australia, on 6 January 1856. [Rattray gravestone]

STEWART, JOHN, of Kinnaldy, shepherd to the 7th Duke of Atholl, emigrated to New Zealand in 1863. [NRS.NRAS.234.6478/3]

STEWART, MARGARET, daughter of William Stewart in Cordon, Perthshire, married William Grant in Montreal, Quebec, on 14 September 1869. [S.8170]

STEWART, MARY, a spinster, from Blair Atholl, emigrated via Fort William aboard the <u>Dove</u> bound for Pictou, Nova Scotia, in June 1801. [NRS.RH2.4.87.73-75]

STEWART, NIEL, from the Bridge of Tilt, in America in 1782. [NRS.CS17.1.1/290]

STEWART, NEIL, from Urrard, died in Tobago on 13 June 1808. [SM.70.718]

STEWART, PETER, born 1757, a labourer from Blair, with his wife Ann born 1757, daughter Ann born 1792, son John born 1795, and son Neil born 1798, emigrated aboard the <u>Clarendon of Hull</u> bound for Prince Edward Island in August 1808. [NSARM] [TNA.CO226.23]

STEWART, PETER, born 1787 in Perth, a mason who emigrated to America via Guernsey, was naturalised in New York on 25 January 1827. [N.Y. Court of Common Pleas Records]

STEWART, PETER, born 1787 in Perthshire, emigrated to Nova Scotia in 1804, died 21 April 1832. [Creighton cemetery, Upper Mount Thom, Pictou County, NS]

STEWART, RANDALL, born 1756 in Callander, emigrated with his wife Margaret Smith to America in 1806, settled in Buncombe County, North Carolina, later in Bibb County, Georgia, died there in 1844. [NCSA.2.103]

STEWART, ROBERT, son of James Stewart of Urrard, a Lieutenant of the 61st Regiment, died in Martinique on 28 June 1795. [CM.11597]

STEWART, ROBERT, born 1791, a labourer from Callendar, emigrated via Port Glasgow aboard the <u>Favourite of St John</u> bound for St John, New Brunswick, on 22 October 1815. [PANB.ms.RS23E.fo.9798]

STEWART, ROBERT, in Gleneagles, Blackford, victim of assault in 1822. [NRS.AD14.22.58]

STEWART, ROBERT, a weaver in Dunblane, was accused of housebreaking in 1834. [NRS.AD14.34.250]

STEWART, ROBERT, a dyke builder in Balnamadoch, , Strathtummel, was accused of the culpable homicide of James Stewart in 1837. [NRS.AD14.37.162]

STEWART, SUSAN A. J., daughter of Colonel Stewart of Fincastle, married Dr Duncan Robertson of Friendship, St Elizabeth, Jamaica, on 23 November 1818. [S.98.18]; Duncan, of Carronvale and Friendship, Jamaica, died in Edinburgh on 12 February 1824. [DPCA]

STEWART, THOMAS, at Bridgend of Callendar, found guilty of assault and imprisoned for eight months in 1819. [NRS.JC11.60]

STEWART, THOMAS, in Forgandenny, a victim of assault in 1824. [NRS.AD14.24.68]

STEWART, THOMAS, in Kirkstile of Auchterarder, a victim of housebreaking in 1825. [NRS.AD14.25.45]

STEWART, WILLIAM, in Cuba, brother of John Stewart in Crieff, testament, 1791, Comm. Edinburgh. [NRS]

STEWART, WILLIAM, a writer in Perth, dead by 1814, brother of James Stewart in Jamaica. [NRS.S/H]

STEWART, WILLIAM, from Grandtully, son of William Stewart a farmer in Stanley, was educated at Marischal College, Aberdeen, in 1849, graduated MB in 1852, and MD in 1853. [MCA]

STEWART, WILLIAM, born in May 1831 in Foss, was educated at the Universities of St Andrews and Edinburgh, a minister in Nova Scotia from 1863 to 1905, died on 26 May 1920. [F.7.618]

STEWART, Miss, daughter of Thomas Stewart of Steeland, married James Arnott, a merchant in Philadelphia, Pennsylvania, in New York in 1808. [SM.70.556]

STIRLING, CHARLES MORAY, of Abercairney, letters of tack to his tenants there, 1805 to 1818. [NRS.GD241.677]

STIRLING, ELEANOR, eldest daughter of ...... Stirling in Comrie, married Robert Campbell of the Hudson Bay Company, in Norway House, North America, on 4 August 1859. [W.XX.2132]

STIRLING, JAMES, ground officer in Blackford in 1818. [PKA.B59.38.5.58]

STIRLING, WILLIAM, an architect in Dunblane, a decreet, 1837. [NRS.CS46.1837.12.169]

STOCHS, DAVID, in Milnathort, Kinross, in 1801. [NRS.CS236.S.10.4]

STOCKS, JAMES, in Perth, died 27 February 1857, father of Jeannie Stocks and Jessie Stocks, both in Hamilton, Canada, [NRS.S/H]

STOCKS, JEDIDIAH, in Perth, died 23 February 1849, uncle of Jeannie Stocks and Jessie Stocks, both in Hamilton, Canada, [NRS.S/H]

STODDART, ALEXANDER, in Meikle Kinnaird, Forgandenny, had his horses stolen in 1830. [NRS.AD14.30.101]

STRACHAN, ELIZABETH, wife of David McLaggan a lawyer in Blairgowrie, was found guilty of reset and sentenced to 12 months in Perth Tolbooth in 1814. [NRS.JC26.1814.14]

STRACHAN ISABELLA, daughter of the late John Strachan in Kinross, a bond of caution re maintenance of her child, the son of Robert Pitcairn in 1819. [NRS.GD1.675.87/96]

STRACHAN, WILLIAM, born 1820, a calico printer in Perth, guilty of housebreaking and theft, was sentenced to transportation to the colonies, on 10 September 1833. [PKA.B59.26.11]

STRONACH, JAMES, born 1793, second son of Reverend William Stronach in Marnoch, a surgeon who died in Bridge of Earn in 1817. [AJ.17.6.1817]

STRONG, ALEXANDER, born 1859, son of Alexander Strong, [1824-1899], in Blairgowrie, died in Chicago, Illinois, on 22 July 1893. [Bendochy gravestone]

STRONG, DUNCAN, born 1776 in Perthshire, a grocer who emigrated via Greenock to America, a baker on Front Street, New York, in 1812, and was naturalised in New York on 18 April 1821. [N.Y. Court of Common Pleas Records] [1812]

STRONG, PETER, born 1821, son of James Strong and is wife Grace Ramsay, died in Iowa on 19 February 1899. [Bendochy gravestone]

STUART, D. M., son of Alexander Stuart [1760-1838] and his wife Janet, [1795-1848], a minister in Dunedin, New Zealand. [Kenmore gravestone]

STUART, JAMES, born 1796 in Perthshire, died 16 November 1857, husband of Janet Stewart, [1800-1875] [North Lochaber cemetery, Antigonish county, NS]

STUART, ROBERT, born 19 February 1785, in Perthshire, son of John Stuart and his wife Mary Buchanan, emigrated to Montreal, Quebec, in 1807, a fur trader, died 29 October 1848. [WA]

SUTHERLAND, SPENCER, a harbour and road contractor in Blairgowrie in 1845. [NRS.CS280.31.63]

SYME, DAVID, son of William Syme in Damhead, Arngask, a victim of assault in 1837. [NRS.AD14.37.164]

SYME, WILLIAM, jr, son of William Syme in Damhead, Arngask, a victim of assault in 1837. [NRS.AD14.37.164]

SYME, JOHN, cashier of the Perth Union Bank, a letter of horning against Robert Pitcairn of Burleigh in 1816. [NRS.GD1.675.34-37]

SYME, WILLIAM, a merchant in Auchterarder, dead by 1853, father of David Syme the Principal of Brooklyn Public School, New York. [NRS.S/H]

SYMON, CHARLES, servant to Jean Rutherford of Glendevon, a victim of assault in 1822. [NRS.AD14.22.58]

TAINSH, CATHERINE, daughter of David Tainsh in Abernethy, a victim of crime in 1823. [NRS.JCC26.1823.198]

TAINSH, or SCOBIE, CATHERINE, in Auchterarder, dead by 1830. [NRS.S/H]

TAINSH, ROBERT DOUGLAS CLARKE, son of Robert Tainsh a surgeon in Crieff, settled in Demerara before 1841. [NRS.S/H]

TAIT, CHRISTIAN, born 1780, a beggar in Dunblane, was accused of theft in 1824. [NRS.AD14.24.74]

TAIT, JAMES, a shepherd in Balado, father of Maggie C. Tait, who married John F. Johnson, at Waltham, La Salle County, Illinois, on 17 February 1875. [S.9876]

TASKER, GEORGE, son of Robert Tasker a farmer in Mawhill, Kinross, died in Palo, Iowa County, Michigan, on 24 January 1864. [DPCA.4191]

TAYLOR, ALEXANDER, born 1825, son of Peter Taylor and his wife Isabel Drummond, died in Australia on 21 April 1860. [Monzievaird gravestone]

TAYLOR, ISABELLA, from Crieffvechter Farm, Crieff, settled in Sydney, Australia, a letter, 1849. [NLS.Acc.13292]

TAYLOR, JANET, in Auchterarder, dead by 1850, aunt of James Taylor a mason in New York. [NRS.S/H]

TAYLOR, JOHN, farmer at Muirhead of Tullibardine, was granted a charter of land in Blackford in 1814. [NRS.GD24.1.93.2]

TAYLOR, JOHN, son of John Taylor a farmer in Blackford, was educated at Marischal College, Aberdeen, in 1842. [MCA]

TAYLOR, JOHN, probably from Perthshire, settled in Reach, Canada West, by 1848. [NRS.GD112.61.5/2]

TAYLOR, MICHAEL, from Perth, emigrated via Belfast aboard the brig Shannon bound for New York on 18 January 1816.

TAYLOR, SUSAN, in Auchterarder, dead by 1850, aunt of James Taylor a mason in New York. [NRS.S/H]

TAYLOR, THOMAS, in Auchmore in Glenshee of Logie Almond, guilty of stealing sheep, was banished, at Perth on 22 September 1797. [PKA.B59.26.11.2]

TAYLOR, THOMAS, in Tibbermuir, a deed, 1806. [PKA.B59.28.200]

THOMSON, FRANCIS H., born 1822, a surgeon from Callendar, died at the Cameroon River, West Africa, on 5 January 1845. [W.563]

THOMSON, GEORGE, a manufacturer in Collace, 1844. [NRS.CS280.30.109]

THOMPSON, JAMES, born 1782 in Perthshire, a merchant in Charleston, South Carolina, was naturalised on 7 July 1800. [NARA.M1183.1]

THOMSON, JAMES, in Milnathort, Kinross, a letter, 1844. [NRS.GD247.292]

THOMSON, JOHN, a farmer from Kinclaven, later in Haughs of Strathord, Ontario, by 1867. [PKA.B59.38.6.6.289]

THOMSON, PETER, born 1824, son of Peter Thomson and his wife Catherine, a merchant in San Francisco, California, died in Oakland, California, on 9 August 1901. [Milnathort gravestone, Kinross]

TOD, DAVID, farmer in Wester Dron, 1850. [NRS.CS313.377]

TOD, WILLIAM, born 9 February 1842, son of William Tod and his wife Agnes Roger, died 6 March 1906 in New Zealand. [Milnathort gravestone, Kinross]

TORRANCE, CHARLOTTTE, widow of Reverend James Wemyss in Orwell, Kinross, 1850. [NRS.CS313.842]

TOSHACH, ALEXANDER, born 1834, son of James Toshach and his wife Isabel Stewart, died in New Zealand in 1889. [Dron gravestone]

TOSHACH, DAVID, labourer in Westerton of Pitgober, Muckart, in 1827, accused of housebreaking and theft in 1827, outlawed. [NRS.AD14.27.168; JC26.1827.168]

TOUCH, JOHN GRAY, from Kinnoull, was educated at King's College, Aberdeen in 1842, joined the Indian Army. [KCA]

TRAIL, JOHN, master of the Alexander of Perth trading between Inverness and Sligo in Ireland, in 1814. [NRS.E504.17.8]

TRAPP, ELIZA, wife of Thomas Barker in Botany, Sydney, Australia, daughter of Michael Trapp a fishmonger in Perth, 1851. [NRS.S/H]

TROTTER, ROBERT KNOX, in Ballindean, Inchture, was accused of administering drugs to procure an abortion in 1842. [NRS.AD14.42.473]

TROTTER, W., in Ballindean, Inchture, a letter to Lord Melville, in 1820. [NRS.GD51.5.332]

TULLOCH, JOHN, moderator of the Free Presbytery of Breadalbane at Logerait a petition, 1846. [NRS.GD112.51.209]

TULLOCH, PATRICK, from Callander, emigrated via Fort William aboard the Dove bound for Pictou, Nova Scotia, in June 1801. [NRS.RH2.4.87.73-75]

TULLOCH, Reverend WEIR, in Tibbermuir, was accused of forgery in 1845. [NRS.AD14.45.212]

TURNBULL, ANDREW, son of John Turnbull an inspector in Perth, was educated at Marishal College, Aberdeen, in 1844. [MCA]

TURNBULL, GEORGE, born in Perthshire, an Ensign of General Marjoribanks Scots Regiment, discharged in 1756, then an officer in the 60$^{th}$ [Royal American] Regiment from 1756 to 1772, later in the New York Volunteers, settled in New York in 1788, died in Bloomingdale on 13 October 1810. [ANY]

TURNBULL, GEORGE, born 1757 in Perthshire, an officer of the Royal Navy, settled in New York in 1783, a Director of the Bank of New York in 1800, died there on 13 November 1825. [ANY]

TURNBULL, THOMAS, in Antigua, son of Catherine Turnbull in Perth, testament, 1817, Comm. Edinburgh. [NRS]

TYRIE, CHARLES, in Dunkeld, cession bonorum, 1832. [NRS.CS236.T9.6]

URQUHART, JOHN, son of Donald Urquhart a porter in Perth, a quarry labourer in Perth, accused of theft in 1830. [NRS.AD14.30.21]

VALANCE, ALEXANDER, was tried for housebreaking and theft in Auchterarder, found guilty, and sentenced to transportation to the colonies for seven years in 1825. [NRS.JC26.1825.288]

WADDELL, ALEXANDER, a travelling chapman, a thief who was sentenced to transportation to the colonies for life at Perth on 8 May 1789. [AJ.2158]

WALKER, EDWARD, probably from Perthshire, settled in Reach, Canada West, by 1848. [NRS.GD112.61.5/2]

WALKER, ROBERT, in Woolmill of Dunblane, a sequestration petition, 1845. [NRS.CS279.2828]

WALKER, THOMAS, a surgeon from Kinross, married Jean McAra, eldest daughter of James McAra a merchant in Largs, Ayrshire, in St Thomas, West Indies, in 1813. [EA.5134.13]

WALLACE, DAVID, in Flatfield, Errol, was accused of assault in 1831. [NRS.AD14.31.56]

WALLACE, JAMES, born 1790, a labourer from Craigenfearn, Logerait, emigrated via Greenock aboard the <u>William of New York</u> bound for New York, landed there on 17 October 1817. [NY Municipal Archives] [NY Commercial Advertiser]

WALLACE, JAMES, son of James Wallace a glazier in Perth, was apprenticed to David Mackie a coppersmith in Perth for six years in 1815. [NRS.GD1.427.16/13]

WALLACE, PETER, a shoemaker in Dunkeld, accused of assault in 1820. [NRS.AD14.20.143]

WARDEN, EDWARD, a writer in Coupar Angus, a trustee in 1802-1803. [NRS.CS96.706.1]

WATSON, CHRISTINE, daughter of Robert Watson in Gelvin, Kinross, accused of theft in 1818. [NRS.AD14.18.177]

WATSON, JAMES, a manufacturer in Errol, dead by 1816. [NRS.CS40.21.38]

WATSON, PETER, born 1858, son of Peter Watson and his wife Janet Paton, died in Paterson, America, on 21 August 1889. [Milnathort gravestone]

WATSON, ROBERT, born 1821 in Perthshire, died in Halifax, New Brunswick, on 31 December 1842. [Acadian Recorder, 31.12.1842]

WATSON, WALTER, born 1821 in Perthshire, died in Halifax, Nova Scotia, on 23 December 1842. [Acadian Recorder, 31.12.1842]

WATSON, WILLIAM, imprisoned in Perth Tolbooth accused of theft in 1820. [NRS.JC26.1820.13]

WATT, ANDREW, son of Andrew Watt a mason in Perth, a merchant who settled in America by 1806. [NRS.CS17.1.25/493]

WATT, JAMES, born 1748, brother of Hugh Watt in Perth, died in Charleston, South Carolina, on 13 July 1833. [AJ.4471]

WATT, JAMES, son of Hugh Watt, a baker in Perth, and his wife Ann Cook, settled in Charleston, South Carolina, died 19 September 1811. [Perth, Greyfriars, gravestone]

WATT, THOMAS, a weaver in Causewayside, Coupar Angus, was accused of discharging firearms there in 1828. [NRS.AD14.28.312]

WEBSTER, JAMES, son of James Webster of Balruddery, married Margaret Wilson, daughter of George Wilson, Harvey Cottage, Nichol, Upper Canada, on 6 March 1838. [AJ.4714]

WEDDERSPOON, ELIZABETH, in Auchterarder, died 9 November 1849, aunt of David Wedderspoon in Otsego, New York. [NRS.S/H]

WEDDERSPOON, HERBERT, a farmer in Otsego, New York, grandnephew and heir of Andrew Wedderspoon a surgeon in Auchterarder who died in 1834, and grandson and heir of James Wedderspoon a teacher in Blackford who died in 1831. [NRS.S/H.1888]

WEST, WILLIAM, schoolmaster in Coupar Angus in 1834. [NRS.CS271.420]

WHYTE, ALEXANDER, a manufacturer in Dunblane, sederunt book, 1816-1818. [NRS.CS96.3561], also a partner in the Allan Flax Spinning Company.

WHITE, ELIZABETH, from Perth, guilty of infanticide, was sentenced to transportation to the colonies for fourteen years in 1799. [PKA.B59.26.11.2; JC11.44]

WHYTE, JAMES, born 1795, son of Robert Whyte a farmer in Muthill, was educated at Glasgow University in 1810, a minister in Salem, New York, from 1825 until his death on 3 December 1827. [MAGU][UPC]

WHITELAW, JAMES, died in Pietermaritzburg, Natal, South Africa, in 1874. [Wellshill gravestone, Perth]

WHITSON, JAMES, in Isal Park, Coupar Angus, a victim of theft in 1848. [NRS.AC14.48.421]

WHITTET, ROBERT, born 1828, son of James Whittet a painter in Perth and his wife Elizabeth Jackson, died on 25 August 1908, buried in Hollywood cemetery, Richmond, Virginia. [Perth, Greyfriars, gravestone]

WHITTET, THOMAS, born 1840, son of James Whittet a painter in Perth and his wife Elizabeth Jackson, died in Montreal, Quebec, on 24 February 1874, [Perth, Greyfriars, gravestone]

WHITTON, PETER, and his wife Helen Isles, parents of Wilfred Smith, born 8 May 1863, died in Denver, Colorado, on 27 July 1900. [Methven gravestone]

WHYTOCK, JOHN, a weaver in Perth, died in March 1825. [NRS.S/H.1878]

WILKIESON, WILLIAM, a housebreaker and thief, was sentenced to transportation for fourteen years at Perth in 1829. [PKA.B59.26.11.3]

WILLIAMS, LINDSAY, a carrier, guilty of forgery, was sentenced to transportation for life, at Perth in 1832. [PKA.B59.26.11.3.6]

WILLIAMSON, ANDREW, in Abernethy, a petition, 1845. [NRS.GD112.51.189]

WILLIAMSON, JOHN, of Meiklour, born 1801, late of New York, died in Blairgowrie on 9 August 1871. [Lethendy gravestone]

WILSON, GEORGE, son of David Wilson a merchant in Coupar Angus, a surgeon in South Carolina, probate 14 January 1791, S.C.

WILSON, GEORGE, in Dunning in 1801. [NRS.CS234.SEQN.W1.19]

WILSON, GEORGE, on the Muir of Kinross, accused of shooting and assault in 1829. [NRS.AD14.29.307]

WILSON, JAMES, born 1828, son of James Wilson and his wife Elizabeth White, died in Australia in 1848. [Newburgh gravestone]

WILLSON, JOHN, in Forgandenny, letters, 1823-1826. [NRS.GD192.28.87-89]

WILSON, JOHN, a weaver in Crieff, accused of being a housebreaker and thief in 1834. [NRS.AD14.34.317]

WILSON, WILLIAM, born in Perthshire around 1794, a tavern keeper, died in Montreal or Quebec on 18 June 1832. [GA.4258]

WINTER, MARGARET, in Perth Tolbooth accused of theft and reset, sentenced to twelve months in prison, 1819. [NRS.JC26.1819.85]

WRIGHT, GILBERT, assistant teacher in Perth Academy in 1803. [PKA.B59.24.6.134]

WYLIE, DAVID, born 1819, a farm servant in Baigley, Dron, accused of poaching in 1836. [NRS.AD14.36.457]

YOUNG, ALEXANDER, born 1785, a labourer from Methven, emigrated via Greenock aboard the Pitt bound for New York on 14 September 1803. [NLS.ms1053]

YOUNG, ANDREW, a travelling chapman in Kinross, was accused on the murder of George Beath near Kinross on 28 July 1802. [NRS.JC26.1803.14]

YOUNG, DAVID, a coppersmith in Perth, 1808. [NRS.GD1.427.10]

YOUNG, GEORGE, a plasterer in Perth later in Canada, dead by 1828, father of John Young a plasterer in New York. [NRS.S/H]

YOUNG, JAMES, a clock and watchmaker in Perth, 1795. [NRS.GD1.427.16/5]

YOUNG, JAMES, in Methven, graduated MD from King's College, Aberdeen, on 26 May 1817. [KCA]

YOUNG, JAMES, in Methven, a sequestration petition, 1842. [NRS.CS279.2900]

YOUNG, JAMES, and his wife Fanny Turton, parents of William B. Young, born 1856, who died in California on 2 March 1903. [Blairgowrie gravestone]

YOUNG, JAMES, born 1838, second son of James Young in Methven, died on board the Cycla in Demerara in 1867. [S.7515]

YOUNG, JOHN, from Perth, guilty of theft, was sentenced to transportation to the colonies for ten years in 1799. [PKA.B59.26.11.2]

YOUNG, JOHN, a glover in Perth, died 6 October 1810, father of George Young in Fitzroy, Canada West. [NRS.S/H.1863]

YOUNG, JOHN, a plasterer in New York, son and heir of George Young a plasterer from Perth, later in Canada by 1828. [NRS.S/H]

YOUNG, MARGARET, from Perth, guilty of libel, was sentenced to transportation to the colonies for fourteen years in 1800. [PKA.B59.26.11.2]

YOUNG, WILLIAM, born 1783, a labourer from Methven, emigrated via Greenock aboard the Pitt bound for New York on 14 September 1803. [NLS.ms1053]

www.ingramcontent.com/pod-product-compliance
Lightning Source LLC
Chambersburg PA
CBHW051943160426
43198CB00013B/2281